Jewish Family Education

A Casebook for the Twenty-first Century

by
Rachel Brodie and Vicky Kelman

Cases Written by: Charlene G. Bornstein, Ellen Brosbe,
Marvin Goodman, Janet Harris, Eric Keitel, Vicky Kelman,
Sherry E. Knazan, Lisa Langer, Irene Resnikoff and Andrew Straus

Judy Shulman, Consultant

a project of

The Jewish Family Education Project

Innovation in Jewish Education since 1897
Bureau of Jewish Education
of San Francisco, the Peninsula, Marin and Sonoma Counties
A beneficiary of the Jewish Community Federation
639 14th Avenue San Francisco, CA 94118
tel 415.751.6983 www.bjesf.org

Made possible by a grant from
the Bernard Osher Jewish Philanthropies Fund of the Jewish Community Federation Endowment
Fund of San Francisco, the Peninsula, Marin, and Sonoma Counties
to the Jewish Family Education Project

Permissions:

Samuel 12:1-14 from the *Tanakh*. Copyright © 1985, by the Jewish Publication Society. Used by permission.

Kadish D'Rabanan, song lyrics by Debbie Friedman. Copyright © 1988 Deborah Lynn Friedman (ASCAP), published by Sounds Write Productions, Inc. (ASCAP). Used by permission.

Excerpt from THE SABBATH by Abraham Heschel. Copyright © 1951 by Abraham Joshua Heschel. Copyright renewed 1979 by Sylvia Heschel. Reprinted by permission of Farrar, Strauss and Giroux, LLC.

ISBN #1-891662-17-1

Torah Aura Productions• 4423 Fruitland Avenue, Los Angeles, CA 90058
(800) BE-Torah • (800) 238-6724 • (323) 585-7312 • fax (323) 585-0327
E-MAIL <misrad@torahaura.com>
Visit the Torah Aura website at www.torahaura.com

MANUFACTURED IN THE UNITED STATES OF AMERICA

Jewish Family Education
A Casebook for the Twenty-first Century

TABLE OF CONTENTS

–Preface–

Jewish Family Education: What Is It?

Simply put, the first step toward Jewish family education is to get the parents out of the car.

It is the first step in a quiet revolution. It marks the end of the long American Jewish tradition of drop-your-kids-off-for-their-Jewish-schooling.

The following steps involve getting Judaism out of the four walls of the school (synagogue, JCC, summer camp) and back into the car with the family—and then into their homes and real lives with them. Jewish family education strives to bring families and Jewish institutions into a more balanced partnership in the challenge to "Jewish" the next generation.

Practitioners in this new and cutting-edge field have found that parents are seeking "something more" than contemporary American culture has to offer them and their children. We find that Jewish families are seeking community, values, some aspect of spiritual life for the family, and they are serious about wanting to be good families. Parents may experience this as a vague state of unease.[1] Good Jewish family education helps them to meet these needs and also helps strengthen the family as a family by providing an island of quality time and the opportunity to practice patterns of positive communication and interaction (which their busy, crowded daily lives may not allow time for).

The critical attributes of Jewish family education are empowerment and scaffolding. Jewish Family Education covers a wide range of learning opportunities, programs and events that share as their goal empowering Jewish families to take charge of their own Jewish lives, to help Jewish families in their struggle to be, become or remain Jewish families by providing them with the inspiration, information, knowledge, skills and resources it takes to get there. Scaffolding describes the help and support built into every program for families as they stretch themselves Jewishly to reach beyond where they can reach on their own.

The "big Jewish ideas" of our tradition form the core of what Jewish family education has to offer families. Think of the process involved in selecting a gift for someone. Great care, thought and planning go into selecting the gift. When that is done, the decision about wrapping the gift is made. In Jewish family education, the "big Jewish idea" is the gift that is being given to the family. The program in which it is delivered is the equivalent of the gift wrapping.

---

[1] It's important to note that they cannot always identify what they need or how or where to look for what they need. As a result, they don't usually come knocking on educators' or rabbis' doors asking for Jewish family education but when quality Jewish experiences for families are offered, families respond with recognition and enthusiasm

The range of programs that fall into the family education basket is very wide—reading programs for families, a congregational garden, family Torah study, parent-child book (or video) clubs, retreats, Israel trips, hikes, Shabbat dinners, tzedakah projects and more.

Professional Development for Family Educators

Family education requires a new set of skills in addition to the traditional skills we expect of Jewish educators in general. We consider **Jewish**, **Family** and **Education** to be the three strands of which professional development in this area is woven. **Jewish** includes study of traditional Jewish texts and "big Jewish ideas." **Family** includes family systems theory, family life-cycle theory and a familiarity with the current writings in sociology that include aspects of family life and community life in America today. **Education** includes theories and practical skills that can translate the educators' knowledge into the design and implementation of Jewish experiences for families.

Because the inter-generational setting is complex and more unpredictable than the standard classroom setting, the family educator has to have (or develop) a high tolerance for noise and commotion along with the ability to attend to many things happening at once. A family educator also needs to have very flexible knowledge—which means very deep knowledge (in all the three areas outlined above). A shallow layer of knowledge will not make one flexible enough to answer questions from adults and kids of widely divergent ages, comfortable with the various social dynamics or able to respond to the many surprising situations that can arise.

In the "phasing in" stages of family education at a site, it is important to work toward dissolving the air of suspicion with which teachers and parents have long regarded one another. And it is important to keep in mind that approaching parents with the same ease that they have with children is often a major hurdle for life-long teachers of children.

We have also found that a background in camping or other non-formal education is often very helpful in acquiring the approach to the type of educational programming that family education requires.

Common Ground: A Learning Conversation for Family Educators

Common Ground: A Learning Conversation for Family Educators was established with a grant to the Jewish Family Education Project[2] from the Bernard Osher Jewish Philanthropies Foundation. It began with eleven participants and met monthly for two and a half hours. (The length of the seminar was in and of itself revolutionary at the time because conventional wisdom held that Jewish educators couldn't [or wouldn't] concentrate for more than an hour and a half at a time.)

It was a two-year cycle with most educators taking year one and then year two, but many also joining for year two and then year one. The number of participants grew to sixteen the second year and then to twenty-two for the third and fourth years. The structure of the seminar evolved as we went along, from one seminar in years one and two to two parallel seminars in year three. In year four we have had one large group seminar one month, followed by two parallel smaller seminars ("sections") the next month. The case was introduced in the large group seminar, and then the smaller parallel sections would have an opportunity to delve more deeply into the case. Over the years the length of the seminar also grew, to three hours in the third year and then to three and a half hours in the fourth year.

The guiding theory of *Common Ground* is that educators can generate their own professional knowledge when guided to think reflectively about their own practice and the practice of others. We have tried to help them develop a stance of inquiry toward their own practice. Journal writing is an important tool in developing the habit of reflection. We built journal writing time into each seminar, setting aside time at the beginning and at the end of each seminar to do this. We have urged participants to develop the habit of journal writing between seminars (but this has proved a difficult discipline for them to make part of their routines, so that most of the journal writing was done in the seminar setting [at the beginning and at the end of each seminar]).

The structure of the course is true to the three-fold structure outlined above. It is built around Jewish, Family and Education.

- **Jewish:** Text study occupies the first hour of every seminar. For the most part we have chosen to study our texts *hevruta* style, providing participants with short texts and guiding questions that they study in small groups of twos and threes for as long as half an hour. Following this, the whole group comes together to consider additional aspects of the text. The choice of *hevruta* style was guided by our strong feeling that this was the best way to empower the educators to feel competent to handle a text that was new to them. In addition, we felt it provided the most powerful model for how they were most likely to structure text study for the families they work with.

---

[2]The Jewish Family Education Project is part of the Bureau of Jewish Education a beneficiary of the Jewish Community Federation of San Francisco, the Peninsula, Marin and Sonoma counties

- **Family:** In year one of the cycle we read articles (academic and popular) about the life of families in America today and studied aspects of family systems. In the second year of the cycle (which is built around cases) many of the cases we studied prompted deep discussion about the families we work with, mostly drawing on the experience of participants—intermarried families, single-parent families, quirky families, stressed-out parents, reluctant participants and so on.

- **Education:** In year one we read articles about education both general and Jewish. During the second half of year one the participants worked together in a kind of "lab" setting to create a program for families built around a "big Jewish idea" which they then were able to try out at their sites.[3] In year two the cases provided many opportunities for discussing a range of practical considerations affecting programming and educational decision-making. We also tried to set aside time for a "Jam Session" at each seminar during which participants could present a practical family education problem in their current practice with which they wanted the group's help.

A typical *Common Ground* session looked somewhat like this:

Journal writing (10 minutes)

Text study (60 minutes)

Family education (year one) / case study (90 minutes)

Jam session

Journal (reflections on day's discussion) (10 minutes)

Wrap-up of loose ends (10 minutes)

Other important details:
- We always served a pretty generous breakfast.
- Participants sat around a table at which everyone could see everyone.
- We (audio) taped each session so that when someone missed a seminar, it would be easy to listen to the seminar and catch up. (We mailed the tapes out to anyone who missed a session.)

The Case Writing Seminar

The case writing seminar was a professional development opportunity for our staff and a select group of educators with some experience working with families.

The seminar took place in the fall of 1997. It brought together the staff of the Jewish Family Education project and dozen educators. They were brought together by a grant from the Bernard Osher Jewish Philanthropies Foundation to the Jewish Family Edu-

---

[3] The first year's seminar designed a family "travel curriculum" to accompany their summer vacation travels which was built around the concept *Mikadesh Hol*, (seeing the holy in the ordinary). The third year seminar developed two site-based family experiences—one designed around *G'milut Hasadim* (acts of loving kindness) and one based around *Derekh Eretz* (common decency toward humanity).

cation Project of the Bureau of Jewish Education of San Francisco, Marin, the Peninsula and Sonoma.

The idea for the project came from discussions with Judy Shulman, a nationally known author and consultant in the area of case methods in the world of general education and a member of the advisory committee of the Jewish Family Education Project from its inception. As our own thinking advanced about the potential power of cases in professional development settings, we realized that Judy would be the perfect consultant to guide our work because she knew the case-writing field and had become quite familiar with the field of family education.

Judy and the twelve case writers (two of whom were staff members) participated in a day and a half residential retreat together which was followed a month later by a one-day retreat in the city. Over the first day and a half we studied a case together[4] that consisted of reading, analyzing and discussing the issues in the case itself. We followed this by putting our own learning experience with the case under a microscope to investigate what we had learned from the way we had learned. This gave us first-hand insight into a way of learning that was new to all of us, as it would be to the people who would study these cases with us.

We began writing our own cases right away—beginning with a fifteen-minute writing stretch after which we shared our writing with the group and were guided to think more sharply by the group's questions. The remainder of the retreat included increasing amounts of time spent writing on our own followed by feedback sessions in pairs or triads. By noon of the second day we all had drafts of cases which we were committed to proceeding with. In the month that followed we each re-wrote and re-wrote and brought our almost finished product to a one-day in-city retreat. At that retreat we listened and polished and came to the completion of the writing process feeling we had a set of ten well-written and varied cases.

It's important to note that the retreat accomplished more than the creation of this product. It proved to be an important professional development experience for all who were involved. We all developed a new way of examining our own work and often thereafter would say, "I see cases everywhere." Or "It helped to ask myself, 'what is this a case of?' when I was stuck." The writing of the cases was valuable for the professionals at the retreat even if the cases had never seen the light of day.

And then?

By the following year we had decided to use the cases as the core of the curriculum for the second year of Common Ground. Over the past three years, all of the cases have had at least one "test run" with family educators—at Common Ground, at the Whizin Institute's summer intensive and in several other professional development settings across the country.

---

[4]As there were no cases in family education, we needed a case to "prime the pump," and felt it would be better to develop a case in family education rather than using one of the cases about group-work or diversity issues that we had at hand. Vicky Kelman, director of the Jewish Family Education Project, working closely with Judy Shulman over several weeks, wrote this first case. It is one of the cases in the collection.

It was during that year that we commissioned the commentaries from family educators outside of our community. Again, this was at the suggestion of Judy Shulman, who had added commentaries to some of her case-study books. We saw this as a way of expanding and deepening the conversation by adding more voices to the discourse.

And now?

It is our hope that this set of commentaries, now in book form, can play a central role in the professional development of family educators. In cities and on campuses where professional development for family educators takes place, this book of cases can serve as a textbook. Individual family educators without a community to study with can learn a lot by working through the book on their own. We are excited to realize that what began as a professional development opportunity in our community is in a form that can be shared so it can play a national role in the development of our profession.

–Casebook Overview–

> Only if we think well to discover what the actual problem is can we move towards a solution, says Dewey in *Reconstruction in Philosophy*:
>
> ...a problem well put is half solved. To find out what the problem and problems are which a problematic situation presents to be inquired into, is to be well along in inquiry. To mistake the problem involved is to cause subsequent inquiry to be irrelevant or to go astray.[5]

What is a case?

Our definition of case is: a verbal snapshot of a dilemma in practice written by the person who has experienced the dilemma.

Why cases are important

Because cases capture a slice of real life, they provide a powerful tool for professional development (in both pre-service and in-service settings). A case provides exposure to the texture of the day-to-life of the "practitioner" in a safe space, protected from the winds and storms of the real world of practice. It enables case-students to sharpen their ability to identify the problems that a problematic situation presents. Every case is a "case of" many things at once.

This collection of cases, all of which document dilemmas in family education, can play a role in the education of both experienced and novice family educators. These cases can be part of preparing a beginner to enter this complex field by providing a way to practice analyzing and solving problems and can also serve to deepen the work of someone already "doing" family education by exposing him/her to situations as yet un-encountered as well as an opportunity to re-visit familiar situations and gain deepened understanding of them.

Cases have two main functions.

To teach: Cases are a way of passing on what Lee Shulman calls "the wisdom of practice." They provide a way of learning from experience without having to experience everything firsthand.

To promote reflection: Those who write cases are encouraged to reflect on the dilemmas of teaching in order to tease out and clearly explicate a difficult situation in which they have been caught. For the reader of the case, it brings alive the complex dynamics of real teaching situations. The reader can experience the pulls of the situation and

---

[5] Michael Rosenak (quoting John Dewey) in his article " From Strength to Strength" in Courtyard, Jewish Theological Seminary of America, 1999/2000, page 69.

think through the multiple issues and crosscurrents in such a way that he/she can play out the various possible "solutions" or pathways out of the tangle.

The advantages of a case-based curriculum

Cases have long been a staple of business school and medical school curricula. They are newer to the field of education.

Case-based teaching can prepare novices for the complexities of practice or for deepening the understanding of a more experienced practitioner. Study of theory and principles provide a framework for thinking but "cases illustrate how complex teaching really is....because they tell vivid, moving stories, cases give life and staying power to concepts...Novices learn how to name problems, interpret complex situations and identify decision points and possible consequences."

The commentaries

As a way of extending our learning from these cases, we asked leading practitioners of family education across the country to share their wisdom with us by becoming commentators on our cases. We asked twenty family educators to play Rashi[6] and by doing so to enhance our understanding of the complexities of this field. Each case has a complement of two "Rashis". These incisive and perceptive commentaries illuminate the issues and challenges of the practice of family education in way that expands and deepens the discussion of each of the cases.

These commentaries are very much the personal opinions of the writers and in no way constitute "the" take on a case. For this reason we feel it is crucial that reading of the commentaries follow the group exploration of the case. The educators who work with cases prefer to study them over two sessions, plumbing the issues presented in the case in a group setting before reading the commentaries. A second round of discussion can follow, based on the reading of the commentaries.

Although we began by devoting one session to each case, we quickly found that our groups have preferred devoting two sessions to a case, reading the commentaries between the two sessions. The discussion based on the commentaries adds interesting angles to the second go-round with the case.

Text study

A hallmark of *Common Ground: A Learning Conversation for Family Educators*, the seminar in which we first studied these cases, is that about a third of the three-hour session was devoted to Jewish text study. In the years in which we studied the cases (the second year of the two-year cycle, i.e., years two and four) we tried to select Jewish texts that were related to the case we were about to study. We selected important Jewish ideas that illuminated the case. For example, two texts (one Talmudic and one modern) about Shabbat preceded the discussion of a case in which an educator shares his/her conflict over what to consti-

[6] Rashi is a famous medieval commentator on the Bible whose commentaries are thought to be indispensable to study of the Bible.

tutes quality *Erev Shabbat* programming for families. A text about *tochecha* complements a case in which a participant reprimands the group leader.

The inclusion of text in conjunction with each of the cases is a way of deepening the discussion and bringing the Jewish tradition to bear on some of the issues raised. Text study can be used in the following ways:

1. Before a case is discussed

2. In the middle (if a case is studied over more than one class session a text study can be used at the beginning of the second session)

The text studies we have developed come from a variety of traditional Jewish sources including the Tanach, Rabbinic literature, liturgy, and Hasidic tales. We tried to select texts that complemented at least one significant issue raised by the case. We did not choose these texts because we think they give "a Jewish answer" to the dilemma of the text but rather because they deepened participants' Jewish knowledge and widened their angle of observation. Many of the texts also led to reflection on personal practice and personal experience.

All text studies presented here have a *hevruta* component. *Cheuruta* study is the traditional model of Jewish text study where students are paired (or placed in very small groups). The students are given the text (sometimes with an introduction by the teacher and sometimes without) and a set of study questions. Students read and study together as the teacher circulates among the pairs and pushes them to deepen their discussions.

In our model, *Hevruta* learning is guided by a set of questions, then followed by large group discussion. The latter allowed for some unstructured exchange about the texts and raised additional questions that were held in reserve in order to extend the discussion (rather than reiterate the *hevruta* discussions).

NOTE: *Hevruta* comes from the same root as the Hebrew word for "friend"—*haver*. The idea behind this type of study is sometimes expressed as follows: The Torah is compared to fire. To make fire spark, it takes two sticks rubbing up against each other (Babylonian Talmud, Taanit 7a). *Hevrutot* (pl.) are the pair of learners and the two sticks. They are meant to combine people who enjoy studying together but who do not agree with each other all the time. The intimacy of the pair that studies together regularly is intense and gratifying and should be created with care. For this reason we have found it helpful to assign people to *hevrutot* at the beginning of the year and then after several sessions to let participants choose regular partners. It also works to have *hevrutot* that organize themselves each time. The learning relationship may not go as deep as a permanent *hevruta,* but this approach builds a web or relationships among participants.

–Facilitating
A Case Discussion–

Excerpted from *Facilitator's Guide to Groupwork in Diverse Classrooms: A Casebook for Educators*, edited by Judith H. Shulman, Rachel A. Lotan, Jennifer A. Whitcomb (NY: Teacher's College Press, 1998).

Preparation and Process

Much can be learned just by reading cases. But a good facilitator can expedite that learning by prompting a group to examine the case's issues in ways that readers by themselves might not. Far more than a lecture, case discussion enlivens content and helps participants internalize theory. Still, the idea of facilitating such discussion can be intimidating: when you don't do all the talking, you relinquish authority and therefore can't be entirely sure how the class is going to go.

This concern is heightened when the cases are problem focused—as all these cases are—and the authors are honest about the dilemmas they face in their [situations]...the surprises that occur, and the reflective questions they ask themselves about how they handled the situation. In the pilot test of [these case studies], teachers identified with authors as they struggled to cope with events. The stronger their identification with an author, the more vulnerable they often were during a case discussion because a criticism of the way the author handled a situation was considered a criticism of themselves...."

Preparing to Lead Discussion

Careful preparation is critical to leading case discussions successfully. You'll need a thorough knowledge of the case as well as clear ideas about how best to use the... [annotated lesson plans] to guide the sessions.

Reading the case. To facilitate a discussion effectively, one cardinal rule applies: you must have a good grasp of the case and its nuances....The only way to develop deep familiarity is to read the case several times. The following suggestions will help guide your reading:

- As you begin, take note of your first impression. What excites you? What bothers you? With whom did you relate? Subsequent readings may change your answers to these questions, so it's important to jot down your initial reactions to use as diagnostic tools. Initially they help you gauge your values and empathic response to the case. Later they may be key in helping you understand participants' starting points in the discussion.

- Since each case has many layers of meaning, each reading yields more information and understanding. As you read, ask yourself "What is this a case of?" and

"What are the different ways to interpret this case?" Also note the descriptive words, key phrases, and dialogue used....

- The more perspectives you have on the case, the better equipped you'll be to prompt broad-ranging discussion, thus reinforcing the idea that there is no one "right answer." Try to keep group participation balanced. Should one person's viewpoint tend to dominate, your suggestion of another lens to look through can draw out participants whose knowledge and experience make them identify with the case in an entirely different way.

- Look for pressure or stress points in the case—instances when [an educator]...is confronted by angry...[individuals], puzzled by a dilemma, or experiencing doubt or remorse about his actions. These events serve as teachable moments in the discussion....

- Look for subtle cues....In many of the cases, information about individuals' perspectives is couched in subtle details. The group needs to look beneath the surface of what occurred. What might have happened if the...[family educator] had perceived the [individual] differently? What might the [case writer] have done, and how might the [individual] have responded?

Using the [annotated lesson plans]. [The annotated lesson plans] are resources designed to help you plan each case discussion....Though the teaching notes are structured to help you analyze specific issues and provide examples of probing questions, they are not designed to give you a particular pathway for moving a group through the case. Instead, they are meant to help you make your own plan for discussion, from which you can deviate as you ascertain the group's direction with the discussion. Anticipating this, you can use the notes to identify stages of discussion and plan probing questions that enable participants to view the case through different lenses. Just as you customize case selection and sequence, you'll want to tailor questions to suit the profile of your particular group or school.

Planning the physical space....We have found that a U-shaped arrangement with participants seated at tables on the outside of the U works best. This arrangement enables participants to maintain eye contact with one another during a discussion and allows the facilitator to move within the circle at will.... We also place either a board or an easel with chart paper at the head of the U for recording major points made during the discussion....

Providing adequate time. It takes time to peel away the surface layers of the cases and get to the underlying problems. If you allow two hours for case discussions, you should have adequate time to delve deeply into most of the cases. But what if you have only an hour to an hour and a half? This doesn't mean you shouldn't try to discuss any cases, but you will have to plan your time accordingly....[We always] distribute the case before the actual discussion and ask participants to read it carefully, jotting down questions and noting issues *before class*.

The practice of coming to a session prepared to discuss a case is desirable even if you don't have a time crunch. In pre-service education, teacher educators frequently ask students to prepare a pre-analysis of a case before class and a post-analysis after the discussion. Pre- and post-analyses enable participants and teachers to track how the discussion influenced participants' insights into each case.

If you're pressed for time, it's important to keep one eye on the clock. It's easy to become caught up in one section of the discussion and run out of time before you complete all the parts you had planned. Stopping a discussion before you can bring it to closure is often more harmful than cutting short a particular section midway through the discussion.

Dynamics of the Group Process

A successful discussion requires a climate of trust, acceptance of differing communication styles, and clearly defined roles and ground rules.

Establishing trust. Successful case discussion can take place only in a climate of trust. How can you help ensure that participants feel safe enough to risk exposing their opinions to others' judgment?

You'll need to consider many factors: physical setting, use of space, seating arrangement, your style of leading discussion, and group size. Perhaps most important, however, is the life experience of group members. Each participant brings to the group her personal values, attitudes, and beliefs—both conscious and unconscious....

The clearer the structure and the more secure you are in the role of facilitator, the better the chances of developing a safe climate and productive discussion. Whenever possible, create groups that include individuals with differing life experiences, so participants can learn from each other.

In a group with well-established trust, the case discussion provides diverse participants a chance to reveal more of themselves and be better understood. In some instances a catharsis occurs and must be handled delicately. It is also important for the facilitator to be aware that established roles among members of a given group may create an obstacle to open discussion because of people's fixed opinions about each other.

Communication styles....Case discussion asks us to think about our reactions to characters in the case. The degree to which people are willing to reveal their values or beliefs is often a function of their style of communication.

Some participants will find it easy to talk openly and debate the topics; others won't. Some will be aggressive; others will hold back until they hear the rest of the group's opinions. Some will want to speak first; others will need prodding to speak at all. Some will disagree openly, others indirectly. These styles reflect not only personality, but culture. In classrooms we often subscribe to a particular model of communication—that you speak up when you disagree. However, to some cultures and individuals, it may be inappropriate to express disagreement.

As the facilitator, you must create a...climate which requires encouraging a variety of opinions through questioning and framing differing perspectives for examining the case. It also means watching people's body language so you won't lose the chance when a quiet person is about to say something. You can step in and gently silence interrupters. ("Susan hasn't had a chance to share her ideas about the story, so let's give her that time.")

Rules and roles. To establish a climate that is supportive of meaningful discussion, it's crucial that all participants understand the goals of the discussion, ground rules, and role of the facilitator.

Case discussion goals. A first step in leading a discussion is presenting the goals of the case seminar:

- To frame and reframe problems in each case

- To explore and analyze multiple viewpoints in each case

- To connect issues in the cases with participants' teaching situations and develop a repertoire of strategies to use in dealing with such issues

- To stimulate collaborative reflection and strategic introspection of one's own practice

- To develop collegiality and a shared understanding among participants

Ground rules for participants. Participants must overcome the notion that there is only one acceptable way to analyze each case. Instead, the aim is to foster an ethos of critical inquiry that encourages multiple interpretations, conflicting opinions, and equal participation. Clear ground rules can help set the stage for this kind of discourse:

- Respect each member's contribution and point of view and listen carefully.

- Do not interrupt! Wait for speakers to finish their statements before responding.

Leading the Discussion

Although you may have more expertise than the group you are working with, as *facilitator* you should not assume the role of expert during a case discussion. Rather, your responsibility is to elicit alternative perspectives and help participants analyze them. You should take the stance of an active listener, reflecting by your words and body language that you heard, understood, and accepted what the speaker communicated. You should also have at your disposal a set of probing questions that help expose, clarify, and challenge assumptions and proposed strategies that participants raise during the discussion (see...[annotated lesson plans] for examples of questions).

If members in your group appear to accept ideas before reflecting on different perspectives, you may offer other perspectives for their consideration. Your goal, however, is not to lead them to a specific point of view, but to help them come to their own conclusions....One of the most difficult aspects of leading case discussions—especially for new discussion leaders—is the possibility that participants may leave a meeting with what appears to you to be the wrong point of view. You may feel compelled to give the "correct" answers, as if there is one best solution. Instead, try not to show impatience with teachers' views. Changing beliefs takes time, and being told what to believe is rarely effective. Individuals come with their own set of experiences that help shape their beliefs. They need time to evaluate these during case discussions and later in their [settings].

The Opening

When beginning a new group, remember that group members may need to get acquainted. Field testing showed that allowing time for participants to introduce themselves, or even using a simple icebreaker, sets a comfortable and warm climate and pays off later. If a group is going to meet several times, it is worthwhile to allow substantial time during the first session for getting acquainted, going over rules and roles, and discussing the purpose of using cases in teacher education.

How do you begin a discussion? Your opening questions are important; they set the tone and scope of the entire discussion. Experimenting with ways to make your openings as flexible and participatory as possible should be one of your goals.

One opening approach is to establish facts by asking one or two people to summarize what actually happened in the case, then asking others to join in. Asking for the facts of the case is a comfortable way to enter the discussion because it enables everyone to begin the discussion with a shared sense of what happened and emphasizes the importance of differentiating fact from interpretation. Sometimes, however, participants become frustrated with this exercise and want to jump right in and get to the provocative issues. If this happens, you will have to judge how important it is to establish facts before delving into larger issues. You can always return to the facts by asking factual questions throughout the discussion and referring back to the text periodically to gather evidence.

Another way to open a discussion is to ask participants to work in pairs for five minutes to generate key issues and questions raised by the case and record their results on a board or easel chart paper before fleshing out any issues. (If you want to begin with facts, you can use this approach after the facts have been established.) There are many advantages to this approach: (1) participants can refer to the list during the discussion, making sure that all points were addressed; (2) you and the group acquire a sense of the range of interpretations before discussion begins; and (3) you convey the idea that there are many ways to look at the case, thus ensuring that the discussion doesn't become fixated on a single view. This approach works especially well when you meet with a new or particularly large group because all members become engaged immediately in discussing the issues. The pair work also serves to break the ice for those who are hesitant to talk in large groups and makes them more inclined to speak up in the larger setting than they might otherwise be.

After completing the list of issues and questions, ask the group to decide where they wish to start the discussion. This sends a subtle message that you respect the group's agenda and won't impose your own. Some teachers reported that this gesture was important; it appears to empower some to speak up who might otherwise remain silent.

A third approach to beginning the discussion is to provide a focus question and immediately examine a key issue. If you choose this tactic, be sure to consider your opening question carefully, because it is likely to set the tone for the entire discussion. The advantage of starting with a focus question is that the discussion usually gets off to a lively beginning. The tradeoff is that it may prevent some participants from bringing up their own issues. It may also convey the perception that you have a fixed agenda for the discussion.

Core of the Discussion

Once the initial focus of the discussion is established, we suggest the following discussion components:

- **Analysis.** Analyze the problem(s) from the viewpoints of the different actors in the case, using the notes as a guide to the analysis. Adequate analysis often takes *at least* half the discussion.

- **Evaluation.** Examine the [educator's]...strategies for handling the problem(s).

- **Alternative Solutions.** Generate alternative strategies for handling the problems, making sure to consider the risks, benefits, and long-term consequences of each.

- **Principles of Practice.** Formulate some generalizations about good practice based on this case discussion, prior discussions, teachers' experience, and their prior theoretical understanding.

- **"What Is This a Case Of?'** Moving up the ladder of abstraction, link this case to more general categories; rich cases are, by nature, "of" many things.

Though this pathway appears to be linear, in reality, discussions rarely follow such a straight path. One aspect of the discussion, however, should follow sequentially. We emphasize the necessity of adequately analyzing the issues in the case—from a variety of perspectives—before evaluating how the [educator]...handled the problems and generating alternative strategies. In our experience, educators sometimes make quick judgments and begin generating alternative solutions before adequately analyzing the problems.

In a typical discussion, the initial focus is on the particularities of the case and an analysis of what happened. In the diagnosis of what went wrong, participants' comments often reflect personal experience (particularly if they are experienced teachers) and theoretical understanding....

The effectiveness of the analysis depends to a great extent on your repertoire of questioning techniques that encourage reflection. Different types of questions (e.g., open-ended, diagnostic, challenging, prediction, and hypothetical) serve different purposes. As facilitator, you should be prepared to follow participants' responses with probing questions that deepen their reflection (see Figure 1 for a typology of probing questions). When participants begin to ask questions of one another, rather than continually orienting their remarks toward you, this is a sign of growth among the group.

Ethos of inquiry. One of the most important tasks of the facilitator is to create an ethos of inquiry–a group spirit that is not limited merely to exchanging opinions, but rather leads to substantive teaming. Accomplishing this task requires remembering that the focal point of a case discussion–the personalized narrative–can be both a hook and a pitfall. The detailed individual story draws people in and prompts them to share their own stories.... But this level of discussion can be so absorbing that the group fails to realize that the point is to generate principles, or sets of practices, or new ways of thinking that can be tested across cases and in...[their own settings].

The facilitator's challenge is, first, to build an ample world of ideas for the group to explore, then to move discussion up and down a ladder of exploration: up to higher principles, back down to very discrete practices, then up again–in other words, to repeatedly move from the level of opinion swap to the desired level of applied knowledge. How do you do that? How do you get people to deduce principles from experiences they're discussing, to move away, come back, then generalize again?

- Try not to become emotionally involved in what's being said. You will be more effective if you keep some distance and continually analyze how the discussion is going. Pay particular attention to equitable participation.

- Periodically tie up loose ends, summarize what's been learned, and move along to the next increment. This keeps group members from repeatedly coming back to the same point or digressing so far that their talk no longer relates to the case.

- After evaluating how...[an educator] in the case dealt with a particular problem, ask what alternative strategies...[the educator] could have used and analyze the risks and benefits of each.

- At opportune moments, ask participants to come up with generalizations or principles based on this and other case discussions and their experience. This develops their capacity to transfer what they learn from the analysis of a particular case to similar situations they are likely to meet....

- Bear in mind that you are teaching the skills of case analysis. Ultimately, you are moving participants toward applying what they're learning to their teaching behaviors, but only in-depth analysis allows that learning to occur, and the skills required take time to develop....

The greatest challenge of the case approach is that each discussion is different and takes on a life of its own. At times the discussion may appear at an impasse, or participants may be ignoring information you feel is key to understanding the case's problems or dilemmas. At such times you need to shift the topic. One way is to say you've spent a lot of time discussing a particular topic, then ask about viewing it from another perspective (give an example). Another tack is to play devil's advocate, then introduce the missing issue as a counterpoint. Or you might elicit questions about a quote from the case. Occasionally it may be useful to push ahead a discussion by giving a two- or three-minute mini-lecture based on the [annotated lesson plans] or other scholarly sources. (This can be risky if it is perceived as too directive; it may also limit discussion.) Another strategy is to incorporate activities such as role playing and/or discussion in structured small groups, which can offer a welcome change of pace.

Be sensitive to the possibility that there may be tension between your agenda for a case discussion and the group's. This requires a delicate balance. If you merely follow where the participants want to take the discussion, you abrogate your role as a teacher; but if you stick to your discussion plan without letting participants move in a direction they prefer, you communicate that you are in control and they might hesitate to bring up their issues and concerns. One way to get around this dilemma is to look for opportunities to build on participants' ideas, rather than raising new ideas yourself. Also, remind them that in your role as facilitator, you will challenge their ideas and push them to defend their views, regardless of their position. Ultimately we are trying to move participants from reflection to problem solving and a willingness to investigate their own...practice.

Closing the Case Discussion

Another major challenge is helping participants synthesize and reflect on what they learned from the entire discussion. Participants should have the opportunity to identify new understandings as well as unresolved conflicts and questions before the discussion is over.

One approach is asking participants to reflect on the case and respond to the question "What is this a case of?" This question, which began as a suggestion from Lee Shulman, is the theme that weaves through all our casework. It asks teachers to characterize a particular case in relation to other cases, to their own experience, and to the conceptual or abstract categories with which they are familiar. Shulman suggests that it is a way of encouraging participants to move between the memorable particularities of cases and the powerful simplifications of principles and theory (L. Shulman, 1996).

> ...the key move made in teaching with cases occurs when instructor and students explore the question "What is this a case of?" As they wrestle with this question, they move the case in two directions simultaneously. They connect this narrative to their remembered (personal) experiences or to vicariously experienced cases written or recounted by others, thus relating this particular case to other specific cases. They also connect this narrative to categories of experience, to theoretical classifications through which they organize and make sense of their world. (pp. 208-209)

In our experience, closing a discussion with "What is this a case of?" has been extremely valuable in helping participants move away from the particularities of a specific case and begin to identify the variety of categories that the case represents. Please note that rich cases are usually "of" many things. Often what they are "of" depends upon the nature of a particular discussion and the experience of its participants.

Other ways of bringing the discussion to closure include asking the students to spend a few minutes doing a "freewrite," responding to such questions as: What did you learn from this case discussion? Do you have lingering questions? What part of the discussion did you find most challenging? How can you relate what we discussed to your own experience? Some people appreciate the opportunity to synthesize their thoughts in writing before sharing them with the larger group.

Another approach is to divide the group into pairs to share what they learned, relate it to their own experience, and brainstorm what they would do differently. After the pairs meet, bring the group back together and ask one member of each pair to report key ideas they discussed.

A final tactic is simply to ask what principles and/or generalizations participants can generate from this and other discussions and what questions remain unanswered. Record this information; you may want to compare it with a previous list of principles.

–Participating in a Case Discussion for the Student–

Excerpted from *Introduction to Education Cases for Teacher Problem Solving* by Rita Silverman, William M. Welty and Sally Lyon (NY: McGraw-Hill, 1994).

For most of you this collection will be a new experience in education....Based on the concept of case study developed in schools of business, these cases present stories told by practicing [family educators]...about their experiences. The stories introduce problems [family educators] have encountered and require that students [of family education]...use their analytic and critical thinking skills, their knowledge of educational theory and research, and their common sense and collective wisdom to identify and analyze problems and to evaluate possible solutions.

Deciding for yourself—that is really the heart of case-method pedagogy. It is based on the understanding that the most important learning, the most meaningful learning, the most long-lasting learning comes from the work the learner does on his or her own—active learning.

Problem-solving cases require that the learner be active in both the preparation for class and the participation in class. Your preparation for a case class will not be limited by the normal "I've got fifty pages to read tonight." Instead, it will be determined by how much work *you* want to put into the analysis, by the limitations you put on yourself. Usually the cases can be read in a relatively short time, since few are more than [three] pages long. But for cases to have any lasting educational value, you must expend much more effort than simply reading them. Because these cases are problem-centered, there will be a more or less obvious "presenting problem." But there will be, as well, some more subtle problems, problems the teacher telling the case story may not have recognized. It will be up to you, in your preparation for class, to identify the problems, apply relevant theory, and develop solutions. There will never be one right solution; often there will be many possible solutions. For sure, there will be better or worse solutions, but better or worse will depend on the analysis you used to understand the problem. That analytic process is the heart of case method....

Cases require active learning in the classroom as well. Do not expect your instructor to prepare a neat lecture that summarizes the main points of the case, points out the relevant theory, provides a list of sources, and details the correct solution. Instead, the class will be a discussion. You will be asked questions designed to get you and your classmates to compare and build your individual analyses into a collective one. You will be challenged to defend your analysis and your solutions, to listen to and challenge others, and to take away from this collective process a deeper understanding of the case situation than you, your classmates, or your instructor could ever have done alone.

All of this is designed not only to make you an active participant in your own education but to prepare you for the *real* world of [family education]....That real world is one of constant action, of making decisions day in and day out. Seldom is there time to consult theory; seldom is one situation exactly like another....[Family Educators], therefore, need to be prepared to analyze situations for themselves and to build and evaluate action plans on their own. They need to know how to go to colleagues and friends for help–again, not in seeking the single right answer but in seeking help in problem analysis. They need to learn to take responsibility for the problems encountered in teaching and, by taking responsibility, to develop a proactive attitude toward those problems. In short, they need to develop critical thinking skills for their profession. We believe that case method education provides a basis for developing these skills and for continuing to use them during one's professional teaching career.

How do I prepare a case?

[T]he following are some concrete, step-by step suggestions for case preparation:

1. *Understand the assignment in context.* Your instructor will probably assign one case at a time and include in the assignment some study questions or issues to think about while you are preparing it....So before you begin to read the case, be sure that you understand the overall framework within which the case is being used and the points your instructor may want to emphasize.

2. *Read the case for an overview.* Try reading the case first rather quickly to get a general idea of what it is about: what happened, who the main characters are, what the problems are, and how the issues in the case relate to the overall assignment.

3. *Analyze the case.* Go back and read the case again, this time much more carefully. Begin to try to make sense of the study questions assigned by your instructor. Make notes of main characters and their relationships with each other. Try to understand the problems, both obvious and hidden. Try to understand the point of view of the case; that is, determine who is providing the information. Identify what impact this perspective may have on the information in the case. Make a list of questions you have about the material, and identify any other information you would like to have. At the end of this stage you should have a list of problems and an understanding of the causes of these problems.

4. *Seek outside information.* At this point you might want to turn to outside sources for help in understanding the problems you have identified and to develop solutions....Anything that helps you understand the case better at this point is fair game to use.

5. *Develop solutions.* Ultimately, cases call for solutions to problems, not to determine the one right answer but to focus analysis and to prepare you for a real world of

teacher action and decision making. Relate your solutions to your analysis of the problems. Since there are no perfect decisions, be sure you understand both the weaknesses and the strengths of your solutions. Every good solution has a downside; it may not negate the solution, but you should at least always understand the negatives as well as the positives of what you are proposing. Prepare to argue for your ideas in class....Be ready to take risks....

How do I participate in class discussion?

Thoughtful participation in case discussion has two components: you should state your own informed ideas and analysis, and you should listen actively to the contributions of your classmates. The case class is a learning community; collectively you and your classmates are proceeding toward a more complete understanding of the case situation and possible solutions. No one person can do it all. Your instructor will guide the class toward this collective understanding, but your active participation and active listening are necessary to further this process. You must listen actively in order to understand where the discussion is going and where the group is in the process of the case analysis so that your contributions are relevant to the discussion of the moment.

After the discussion is over, go back over your analysis of the case and think about how the discussion changed or added to it. Try to summarize in a few thoughts the main points of the whole case exercise, from original assignment to summary statement at the end of class. Be sure you understand how and where the case related to theory. Think about the questions you still have relating to the case or the general assignment and about the ways you might begin to answer them.

Case method is an exciting new venture in [family]...education. Our experiences using case method teaching have demonstrated that new teachers go into their own classrooms more ready to deal with the myriad of problems they must face if as students they have prepared seriously for case discussions by taking the time to analyze the cases and to develop solutions based on the educational theory and have taken part in case discussions with both thoughtful contributions and active listening.

–How to Use This Book–

Using the annotated lesson plans

Think of the annotated lesson plans as a recipe. The ingredients are there in a suggested sequence. The recipe and ingredients have been tested and are known to work. The analogy to a recipe implies correctly that as a neophyte with case analysis you would do well to follow the "tried and true." As you become more experienced and more familiar with the ingredients, you will feel freer to experiment with the ingredients and the sequencing and know that you will have a successful outcome for your students.

Of course, the study of cases will be much more of a free-flowing experience than the annotated lesson plans may imply. Even that first step, the retelling of the bare facts (important because people who have read the same case do not always talk as if they have actually read the same case) can sometimes generate its own lively discussion. It helps to get key details clear before moving on into issues. At times you have to rein in your students' interpretive inclinations at this point.

And—once you get past that initial phase and into "what is this a case of?" the discussion will have a tendency to flow rapidly all over the place. Stick with the question ("what is this a case of") and try to have each answer phrased so it answers that question. (We use an easel pad with the heading "this is a case of...." on which we list as many options as the group can come up with.) The trickiest aspect of this part of case analysis is to avoid criticizing the case writer ("he made a big mistake when..." ; "she shouldn't have..."or solving "the" problem. All these cases are legitimately cases of many things. One of the strong assets of case analysis as a form of professional development is that it develops clear thinking about the nature of the problem. This is a skill that educators need in their daily lives. Problems aren't always what they seem. The person who jumps to a conclusion and solves the "problem" in haste may be creating more problems or leaving the real one to fester. "To mistake the problem involved is to cause subsequent inquiry to be irrelevant or to go astray." (Rosenak)

The selection of which issue to tackle first or which issues to tackle in what order can be by consensus, or it can be "instructor's choice." The latter would be made based upon issues that you know are "hot" for the group, as a balance to case discussions that have already taken place or will be coming. Occasionally we have selected three issues that the group feels are important and then divided the group into thirds with each third delving into one issue. (This works well when the group has had several cases they have already studied together.)

How to use the grid

If you're teaching more than one case, you may want to steer participants away from an issue that will be better illuminated in another case.

How to use the commentaries

We always gave the commentaries out to our students to read after the first session devoted to a case for discussion during the second session. It is helpful to cover these points:

• What did these experts bring up that was not mentioned in our discussion?

• Do you agree with their assessments?

• Do they agree with each other?

• Do their comments illuminate the case for you?

Table 1. Overview of Issues Across the Cases

CASE NAME	#1 The Korns	#2 Joey	#3 Daze of Awe	#4 Roadblock	#5 Judith	#6 Alan	#7 The Tallit Project	#8 Shabbat Dinner	#9 Indian Folk Tale	#10 Karen & Sally
A Case of:										
Challenging Family	X	X			X					
Challenging Parent						X			X	
Definition of Family Ed		X		X		X				
Diversity of Jewish Knowledge/Background		X			X	X			X	
Goals for Family Ed	X	X		X	X	X		X		
Group Dynamics	X	X	X		X				X	
Institutionalizing Family Ed				X			X	X		X
Lack of Communication				X			X			X
Participant Motivation		X			X			X		
Planning	X	X	X		X		X	X	X	X
Professional Development										X
School Politics				X			X			X
Subject Matter Knowledge					X				X	
Surprise						X			X	
Teachers of children becoming teachers of adults	X				X					X
Tension between educational and social goals								X		
Tension between personal and professional goals			X					X		
Vulnerability of the Professional	X	X	X	X	X	X	X		X	X
Working in your own community			X	X					X	

TEXT STUDIES, CASES, COMMENTARIES AND ANNOTATED LESSON PLANS

–Introduction to Case Study Through Text Study–

The Parable of Nathan the Prophet

We used this text study as part of a full session devoted to introducing participants to case study. In that session we laid the groundwork for the case study course by comparing case study with parables. We shared some of the information found in the introduction to this book (what is a case, how the cases were developed, how the commentaries were used, etc.).

TEXT: II Samuel, chapter 12:1-14 (Hebrew & English translation)

CONTEXT: The saga of King David is told in the Biblical books I & II Samuel. David's remarkable achievements in the political arena stand in sharp contrast to the failures in his family life. In the story of his involvement with Bathsheva, David reaches a moral low and God sends Nathan, the prophet, to rebuke him. At the start of our text (II Samuel 12) Nathan appears to David on the pretext of seeking advice on a minor but disturbing crime.

Read II Samuel 11 (it can be assigned as homework or read aloud in class) for background then study the parable in depth using the questions (below) to analyze the efficacy of Nathan's approach.

QUESTIONS FOR STUDY IN HEVRUTA

- Why did Nathan use a parable with David?
- What makes the parable so effective?
- What is the value of a parable as opposed to "straight speech"?

LARGE GROUP DISCUSSION POINTS—for the facilitator

Nathan's use of a parable:

- By approaching David with what seems to be a very straightforward legal case, Nathan forces David to see his own behavior reflected in someone else. Until this point David has rationalized his own behavior, but in the face of Nathan's parable he immediately recognizes and acknowledges the wrongs he has committed. By depersonalizing the critique David is able to see the issue's moral simplicity and to express self-condemnation.

Compare and contrast parables and case studies:

- Case studies, like parables, are depersonalized and are therefore useful in forcing us out of our accustomed passivity as readers. Once engaged, the format allows us critical distance to analyze and critique with a minimum of defensiveness and a maximum of empathy. But while parables are meant to have a one-to-one correspondence between the images and the message, case studies are more slippery because they are constructed to match a messier reality. Parables contain their own solutions and are created to convey clear messages, while case studies raise the deep questions that force us to struggle with issues that transcend a specific solution.

Text Study

2 Samuel 12:1-14, or Mashal Natan

12 [1]But the Lord was displeased with what David had done, and the Lord send Nathan to David. He came to him and said, "There were two men in the same city, one rich and one poor. [2]The rich man had very large flocks and herds, [3]but the poor man had only one little ewe lamb that he had bought. He tended it and it grew up together with him and his children; it used to share his morsel of bread, drink from his cup, and nestle in his bosom; it was like a daughter to him. [4]One day, a traveler came to the rich man, but he was loathe to take anything from his own flocks or herds to prepare a meal for the guest who had come to him; so he took the poor man's lamb and prepared it for the man who had come to him."

[5]David flew into a rage against the man, and said to Nathan, "As the Lord lives, the man who did this deserves to die! [6]He shall pay for the lamb four times over, because he did such a thing and showed no pity." [7]And Nathan said to David, "That man is you! Thus said the Lord, the God of Israel: 'It was I who anointed you king over Israel and it was I who rescued you from the hand of Saul. [8]I gave you your master's house and possession of your master's wives; and I gave you the House of Israel and Judah; and if that were not enough, I would give you twice as much more. [9]Why then have you flouted the command of the Lord and done what displeases Him? You have put Uriah the Hittite to the sword; you took his wife and made her your wife and had him killed by the sword of the Ammonites. [10]Therefore the sword shall never depart from your

יב ¹וַיִּשְׁלַ֧ח יְהֹוָ֛ה אֶת־נָתָ֖ן אֶל־דָּוִ֑ד
וַיָּבֹ֣א אֵלָ֗יו וַיֹּ֤אמֶר לוֹ֙ שְׁנֵ֣י אֲנָשִׁ֣ים הָי֤וּ
בְּעִ֣יר אֶחָ֔ת אֶחָ֥ד עָשִׁ֖יר וְאֶחָ֥ד רָֽאשׁ׃
²לְעָשִׁ֗יר הָיָ֛ה צֹ֥אן וּבָקָ֖ר הַרְבֵּ֥ה מְאֹֽד׃
³וְלָרָ֣שׁ אֵֽין־כֹּ֗ל כִּ֣י אִם־כִּבְשָׂ֤ה אַחַת֙
קְטַנָּה֙ אֲשֶׁ֣ר קָנָ֔ה וַֽיְחַיֶּ֔הָ וַתִּגְדַּ֥ל עִמּ֖וֹ
וְעִם־בָּנָ֣יו יַחְדָּ֑ו מִפִּתּ֨וֹ תֹאכַ֜ל וּמִכֹּס֤וֹ
תִשְׁתֶּה֙ וּבְחֵיק֣וֹ תִשְׁכָּ֔ב וַתְּהִי־ל֖וֹ כְּבַֽת׃
⁴וַיָּ֣בֹא הֵ֘לֶךְ֮ לְאִ֣ישׁ הֶֽעָשִׁיר֒ וַיַּחְמֹ֗ל
לָקַ֤חַת מִצֹּאנוֹ֙ וּמִבְּקָר֔וֹ לַעֲשׂ֕וֹת
לָאֹרֵ֖חַ הַבָּא־ל֑וֹ וַיִּקַּ֗ח אֶת־כִּבְשַׂת֙
הָאִ֣ישׁ הָרָ֔אשׁ וַֽיַּעֲשֶׂ֔הָ לָאִ֖ישׁ הַבָּ֥א אֵלָֽיו׃
⁵וַיִּֽחַר־אַ֥ף דָּוִ֛ד בָּאִ֖ישׁ מְאֹ֑ד וַיֹּ֙אמֶר֙
אֶל־נָתָ֔ן חַי־יְהֹוָ֕ה כִּ֣י בֶן־מָ֔וֶת הָאִ֖ישׁ
הָעֹשֶׂ֥ה זֹֽאת׃ ⁶וְאֶת־הַכִּבְשָׂ֖ה יְשַׁלֵּ֣ם
אַרְבַּעְתָּ֑יִם עֵ֗קֶב אֲשֶׁ֤ר עָשָׂה֙ אֶת־הַדָּבָ֣ר
הַזֶּ֔ה וְעַ֖ל אֲשֶׁ֥ר לֹא־חָמָֽל׃ ⁷וַיֹּ֧אמֶר נָתָ֛ן
אֶל־דָּוִ֖ד אַתָּ֣ה הָאִ֑ישׁ כֹּה־אָמַ֨ר יְהֹוָ֜ה
אֱלֹהֵ֣י יִשְׂרָאֵ֗ל אָנֹכִ֞י מְשַׁחְתִּ֤יךָֽ לְמֶ֙לֶךְ֙
עַל־יִשְׂרָאֵ֔ל וְאָנֹכִ֥י הִצַּלְתִּ֖יךָ מִיַּ֥ד
שָׁאֽוּל׃ ⁸וָאֶתְּנָ֨ה לְךָ֜ אֶת־בֵּ֣ית אֲדֹנֶ֗יךָ
וְאֶת־נְשֵׁ֤י אֲדֹנֶ֙יךָ֙ בְּחֵיקֶ֔ךָ וָאֶתְּנָ֥ה לְךָ֖
אֶת־בֵּ֥ית יִשְׂרָאֵ֖ל וִיהוּדָ֑ה וְאִ֨ם־מְעָ֔ט
וְאֹסִ֥פָה לְּךָ֖ כָּהֵ֥נָּה וְכָהֵֽנָּה׃ ⁹מַדּ֜וּעַ
בָּזִ֣יתָ ׀ אֶת־דְּבַ֣ר יְהֹוָ֗ה לַעֲשׂ֣וֹת הָרַע֮
בְּעֵינַו [בְּעֵינַי֒] אֵ֣ת אוּרִיָּ֤ה הַֽחִתִּי֙ הִכִּ֣יתָ
בַחֶ֔רֶב וְאֶ֨ת־אִשְׁתּ֔וֹ לָקַ֥חְתָּ לְּךָ֖ לְאִשָּׁ֑ה
וְאֹת֣וֹ הָרַ֔גְתָּ בְּחֶ֖רֶב בְּנֵ֥י עַמּֽוֹן׃ ¹⁰וְעַתָּ֗ה
לֹא־תָס֥וּר חֶ֛רֶב מִבֵּֽיתְךָ֖ עַד־עוֹלָ֑ם עֵ֚קֶב

2 Samuel 12:1-14

House—because you spurned Me by taking the wife of Uriah the Hittite and making her your wife.' [11]Thus said the Lord: 'I will make a calamity rise against you from within your own house; I will take your wives and give them to another man before your very eyes and he shall sleep with your wives under this very sun. [12]You acted in secret, but I will make this happen in the sight of all Israel and in broad daylight.'"

[13]David said to Nathan, "I stand guiltily before the Lord!" And Nathan replied to David, "The Lord has remitted your sin; you shall not die. [14]However, since you have spurned the enemies of the Lord by this deed, even the child about to be born to you shall die."

כִּי בְזִתָנִי וַתִּקַּח אֶת־אֵשֶׁת אוּרִיָּה הַחִתִּי
לִהְיוֹת לְךָ לְאִשָּׁה: [11]כֹּה | אָמַר יְהוָה
הִנְנִי מֵקִים עָלֶיךָ רָעָה מִבֵּיתֶךָ וְלָקַחְתִּי
אֶת־נָשֶׁיךָ לְעֵינֶיךָ וְנָתַתִּי לְרֵעֶיךָ וְשָׁכַב
עִם־נָשֶׁיךָ לְעֵינֵי הַשֶּׁמֶשׁ הַזֹּאת:
[12]כִּי אַתָּה עָשִׂיתָ בַסָּתֶר וַאֲנִי אֶעֱשֶׂה
אֶת־הַדָּבָר הַזֶּה נֶגֶד כָּל־יִשְׂרָאֵל וְנֶגֶד
הַשָּׁמֶשׁ: [13]וַיֹּאמֶר דָּוִד אֶל־נָתָן חָטָאתִי
לַיהוָה ס וַיֹּאמֶר נָתָן אֶל־דָּוִד גַּם־יְהוָה
הֶעֱבִיר חַטָּאתְךָ לֹא תָמוּת: [14]אֶפֶס
כִּי־נִאֵץ נִאַצְתָּ אֶת־אֹיְבֵי יְהוָה בַּדָּבָר
הַזֶּה גַּם הַבֵּן הַיִּלּוֹד לְךָ מוֹת יָמוּת:

CASE #1
THE KORNS

Text: We Were Strangers

TEXTS: Leviticus 19:33-34 & Deuteronomy 10:18-19 (Hebrew & English translation)

CONTEXT: *Ger* is often translated as "stranger," "alien," or "other." Today the word *ger* is used to mean a person who has converted to Judaism, but in Biblical terms the *ger* was usually a foreign merchant, a craftsman or a mercenary soldier. In the Bible *gerim* are often listed among the disenfranchised whom we need to be reminded to treat well. Part of the Biblical ethos includes empathy with the *ger* based on our own experience as *gerim* (pl.) in Egypt.

LARGE GROUP DISCUSSION POINTS—For the Facilitator:

- We were *gerim*: The Egypt experience, plus God's own example of charitable treatment of *gerim,* is meant to spur us to action. We are expected to incorporate *gerim* into our lives and "love them as ourselves." If this were a natural thing there would be no need to mandate it. In fact, xenophobia and marginalization of "others" seems more instinctive for human beings. And yet, as Jews we are obligated to treat *gerim* with respect, fairness and charity and above all, to extend ourselves to them through empathy. This challenge applies on every level from the national to the interpersonal.

- *Gerim* as metaphor/*gerim* among us. Let us extend the discussion of *ger* to families and individuals who are labeled "other" or "different," those who do not seem to fit into the group. What is our responsibility as Jewish educators to the *ger*? What is our obligation to the larger group? Are these two ever in conflict? What do we do if they are?

Text Study

Leviticus 19: 33-34

"When a *ger* resides with you in your land, you shall not wrong the *ger*. The *ger* who resides with you shall be to you as one of your citizens; you shall love the *ger* as yourself, for you were *gerim* in the land of Egypt: I the Lord an your God."

³³וְכִי־יָגוּר אִתְּךָ גֵּר בְּאַרְצְכֶם לֹא תוֹנוּ אֹתוֹ: ³⁴כְּאֶזְרָח מִכֶּם יִהְיֶה לָכֶם הַגֵּר ׀ הַגָּר אִתְּכֶם וְאָהַבְתָּ לוֹ כָּמוֹךָ כִּי־גֵרִים הֱיִיתֶם בְּאֶרֶץ מִצְרָיִם אֲנִי יְהוָה אֱלֹהֵיכֶם:

Deuteronomy 10:18-19

"Uphold the cause of the orphaned and the widow, and love (befriends) the *ger*, providing the *ger* with food and clothing. You too must love (befriend) the *ger*, for you were *gerim* in the land of Egypt."

¹⁸עֹשֶׂה מִשְׁפַּט יָתוֹם וְאַלְמָנָה וְאֹהֵב גֵּר לָתֶת לוֹ לֶחֶם וְשִׂמְלָה: ¹⁹וַאֲהַבְתֶּם אֶת־הַגֵּר כִּי־גֵרִים הֱיִיתֶם בְּאֶרֶץ מִצְרָיִם:

Case #1: The Korns

Last night I left one Post-it® in a column of its own. This morning that Post-it® and all the others seemed to be staring at me from their columns atop the table. I let out a sigh, dropped my bags and approached the table, as I do every morning during the last few weeks of summer, to look at those Post-its® and gauge my reaction to the different groups.

Each Post-it® represents one of the 75 families enrolled in *B'Yachad*, the Jewish family education program at our congregation. Each column represents a group of eight to ten families who will learn together for an hour each *shabbat* during the coming academic year. Families choose this educational experience instead of the traditional Sunday school, and enrollment is on a first-come, first-served basis. This is a very popular option. Eighty percent of the families enrolled last year are participating again this year, and the remaining spaces fill up quickly. Twenty-five percent of the elementary school-aged children enrolled in our congregation's Judaica programs are in *B'Yachad*.

Organizing the 75 families into groups occupies an enormous amount of my time. Families who choose this program are looking for a Jewish environment in which to learn, grow, have fun and make friends. As director of the program, I want the groups to click because I understand the value added to learning when the members of the group like and respect each other. When I form the family groups, I consider the children's ages and genders; the participants' Jewish knowledge; whether families are returning or new to the program; last year's groupings; friends, interests, parenting styles and learning styles; and, of course, their requests. Complicating this process is the ever-present tension between the goals of the program and the varying expectations of the families. Some families place Jewish learning as their priority, while others place Jewish community as their most important goal. If a family is not in a group with their friends, will they be too disappointed to learn? Will a new family connect with the others in the group? Do the families in a group have similar Jewish knowledge, interest and practice? What about the family that doesn't seem to fit in to any group?

A phone call yesterday threw me off. Carolyn called to request *not* to be in the same group as the Korn family. She had heard that I was organizing the groups and, because two of her children are the same ages as the two Korn children, she knew the odds were high that they would be placed in the same group. After being in the same group with as the Korns last year, she felt that she simply could not spend another year with them. After assuring her that family group assignments were still in flux, and that nothing had been settled, I asked her to tell me more about her request. Her complaints focused entirely on the behaviors and personalities of Mr. and Mrs. Korn—their inappropriate comments and peculiar perspectives, and the inattentive parenting style that had often caused classroom management problems. She suggested that I counsel the

Korns to choose the more traditional Sunday education program rather than *B'Yachad* for the good of the Korn children. My response to Carolyn noted the fact that her objections were based entirely on the Korn parents and not at all on the educational needs of the Korn children. I thanked her for her call and assured her that I would do my best to honor her request and put her family in a group that would meet their needs. I don't think she was satisfied.

After I hung up the phone, I walked over to the table and put the Korns in a column of their own. Carolyn's request was not unexpected. In fact, many people share her feelings about the Korns. I have heard and observed similar negative reactions to them—primarily to the Korn parents—since I came to the congregation three years ago. The Korns have been members of the congregation for many years. Their *havurah* disbanded because other families did not want to spend time with them. On more than one occasion, Mr. or Mrs. Korn has raised unrelated issues during our adult study. They don't always seem to be "on the same page" as everyone else engaged in the discussion. I rarely see them socializing with other adults during the break. Teachers have described activities that work successfully with the other families, but during which the Korns seem to lose their ability to function as a family and tend to retreat to a corner. I have witnessed their younger child throw a tantrum which the parents ignored, leaving the older child to address it. It is as if these parents are missing some parenting and social skills that would enable them to participate fully in family life and, therefore, in this type of program. The Korns seem unaware of their situation and unfazed by their deficient skills. While the Korns' behavior is annoying and disappointing, it has not impacted *B'Yachad* in a way that would preclude their participation. I still hope that spending time with other families will teach them something about appropriate parenting.

Each year a few families enroll in *B'Yachad* who lack social skills and personalities that would add significantly to a group. Yet such families have every right to be in this program, which is open to any member of our congregation. In one version of the columns, I put all those families together, thinking they would cancel each other out. But that seems to be a set-up for doom. So my latest plan is to spread these "square pegs" among the groups and hope they will blend in.

Donna, a thoughtful, perceptive and trustworthy *B'Yachad* parent, passes by my office. I quickly put the Korns into a column and run out to ask her to look at the groups. She is happy to offer her opinions. Her comments are appropriate and her insights are thought-provoking. Together we move a few families, spend some time talking about the enormity of this task and chat about the summer adventures of her family. I thank her for her time and remind her that this is still a work in progress that she should not talk about. I ask if I can call in a few days to solicit her reaction to a future draft. She says, "Of course, but I think you should get others' opinions, too." I assure her that the rabbis have offered input, as have a few other parents and even teachers in the program. Each of their perspectives is helpful and important to this process, but in the end I must make the decisions.

I try to work at my desk, but the Post-its® seem to demand my attention. I feel such pressure to match groups in a way that will maximize our ability to meet our educational and social goals for this program. At some point I will just have to settle on the groups, recognize the potential conflicts and issues that will arise, and work with the teachers on group dynamics. I don't have total control—that should be my mantra.

I feel secure that every *B'Yachad* participant will learn and grow Jewishly. I know that I am doing my best to create an environment where that can happen, but I can't—nor do I think it's helpful to—shield people from uncomfortable, challenging or awkward interpersonal situations. We all deal every day with people we'd rather not encounter. It's a survival skill we must acquire to function in this world. Is *B'Yachad* meant to prepare people to function in our world in a Jewish way? Or is it meant to provide a safe, secure, ideal environment in which to experience Jewish learning?

The program begins in a few weeks, and the Korns' Post-it® will need to be placed permanently in one column or another before long. Every family will be in a group, and every group will have its challenges. Although I am still uncertain about where to place the Korns, the struggle to place them has raised important questions about the process and purpose of Jewish family education:

- What is the right balance of social opportunity and educational content in Jewish family education?

- When there is a conflict between the needs of children and the needs of parents, how should it be resolved?

- How can the goals of this ongoing program be constructed and conveyed so that everyone understands that continually dealing with others is important? This is not a *havurah* program where classes have the same people each year, but one in which switching groups should be expected and eagerly anticipated.

- What is my responsibility as an educator to make everyone happy?

- Should I have a conversation with the Korn family? Should they know about the challenge involved in placing them in a group? Is it my role to intervene in an issue that is clearly bigger than the question of which *B'Yachad* family group they fit into?

- If community-building is a significant goal of Jewish family education, where does a square peg family fit in?

Commentary by Harlene W. Appelman

The first issue that came to my mind when thinking about this case involves the training of Jewish family educators.

Jewish family educators need a variety of skills. Just as Jewish family education must include the Jewish, the family and the education, so must Jewish family educators be grounded in Judaism, family systems and education. Although we expect most Jewish family educators to have a good Jewish background and teaching credentials, we do not always emphasize the necessity of intuitive social work skills (or at least ability in interpersonal communications), particularly with respect to working with families. While they are not therapists, and while they should not engage in intervention work, they do need a lot of experience with "what if" situations (like this casebook) that present interpersonal communications issues and likely scenarios in order to train them in appropriate ways to respond.

The second issue involves expectations of the family educator with respect to families like the Korns. This "square peg family" has insinuated itself into the life of the congregation and the family education program for precisely the reasons that cause such discomfort for their fellow congregants around them. This family unit acts like the children who use what Stephen and Sybil Wolin describe as a "recruiting technique" [1]—finding normal families to adopt them informally because they realize that what is going on in their own families is "not right." These children seek out and attach themselves to families that help them and give them positive family experiences. Families like the Korns, who sense that they have trouble functioning, may seek out and join other groups who can serve as buffers for their problems. What better place is there than the synagogue to hunt for such buffers? Should a family educator get involved in this situation, and if so, how?

There must be support systems in place so that, no matter what happens, the family educator does not have to handle this situation alone. So many times (probably because of the type of teacher/professional that family education attracts) family educators expect to do everything themselves, from planning to shopping to room layout to Post-it® note group analysis. The family educator needs a team and an institutional structure so that, when faced with the square peg family, he/she is not the sole decision-maker. Why is the family educator alone responsible for this program? Where is the professional team that serves as a filter and a support in solving these issues? Where is the lay structure to which the family educator can turn in forming the family groups? Why is the square peg family the topic of discussion in a coincidental meeting with a lay person who happens to be in the hallway?

---

[1] Sybil and Steve Wolin in a presentation to the Whizin Institute for Jewish Family Life, Los Angeles in June 1994.

Families are too fragile and complex to be the sole responsibility of any one professional. The rabbi, the educator and the family educator all should be invested in the success of the families in the congregation. Which professional in this congregation has a relationship with this family? Is there a social worker available from Jewish Family Services, or one that is used routinely in the congregation, with whom this problem could be discussed?

The third issue involves community-building. If that is one of the goals of family education, how do we accomplish that goal?

In the case of *B'yachad*, which responsibilities for this program fall to the family educator, and which can be shared? If this program builds community, why not have a workgroup including the rabbi and some of the teachers take responsibility for forming the groups? Part of community-building entails involving the community in building its own program. In addition, such a workgroup could help design an application process and an orientation session that address some anticipated challenges from the start. When behavior, attendance and group rotation become norms set by the group, decision-making does not become the "job" of any one person (including the professional).

Finally, this case raises the question of how content merges with community. During the group orientation, Jewish texts can be used to address some of these issues. Texts on *bushah* (embarrassment), welcoming the stranger and welcoming guests could serve as part of the learning process. These are life skills about which Judaism has a lot to say and issues that affect not only the parents, but the children as well. The phenomenon of the square peg family is not unique to the synagogue. How do we handle similar situations in our homes? Learning how to deal with such families can help families function better as hosts in their own homes. The *B'Yachad* orientation session can also include getting-to-know-you games and other community-building exercises. Community-building, team-building and Torah all speak to interpersonal issues that occur every year in every family group. Social opportunity and educational content need not be seen as separate categories. Good family education should offer both.

Commentary by Sally Weber

The case of the Korns raises interesting and important issues about the nature of Jewish family education and the responsibility of the educators for keeping everyone at least engaged, if not necessarily always happy.

Most of us have known a family like the Korns—a family that attempts to participate in our programs but, for a variety of reasons, primarily social, just doesn't fit in. Sometimes they are in our family education programs, sometimes in our *havurot*. Invariably, we learn of them when other families come to complain that "they don't fit in," "they're nice but just not appropriate for this group," or "they make us feel uncomfortable."

The dilemma of the family educator faced with such a family has several sources. First, s/he is concerned about both the educational needs of each family and about incentives and barriers to their access to Jewish education. As this case study indicates, social chemistry can be both an incentive *and* a barrier. Second, families bring a wide range of backgrounds, ability, openness, motivation, intellect and social skills to our settings. Not all families are ready for the same thing at the same time. At the same time, an attractive and high-profile family education program may appeal to a wide range of families for very diverse reasons that may or may not be related to the purposes of the program.

Third, and perhaps most difficult for the family educator, family education is not for every family. As this case exemplifies, often families choose to participate in family education programs but, because of their internal social constructs and behaviors, are ill-suited for programs that require certain social skills and conformity to group norms (e.g., around parenting) and families' "clicking" for their success.

In fact, a Jewish family education program cannot be a panacea for all the social/psychological and communal issues that each of our families faces. And while it is admirable to want to create environments where square peg families may learn appropriate parenting from new role models, I doubt that this is an appropriate goal for a family education program.

When a synagogue or school offers a variety of choices for family participation, the professionals have not only a say, but a responsibility to determine which modality best fits the needs and abilities of a given family. A family that is a square peg in one setting may well find success in another. All of us, in certain parts of our lives, are square pegs—which is why we must offer more than one modality for our families.

We must also accept the simple but painful truth: We can't make everyone happy. If that is our goal, we are doomed not only to fail, but to cause a lot of grief. However, as professionals we *can* use our expertise to assess a family's needs and abilities. And we can, with honesty and integrity, explain why one setting may work better for them than others. The Korn family may be disappointed to be told that the *B'Yachad* model is too open and unstructured for their family style and for their children's needs, but a strong educator can interpret their family needs in a positive light and determine if there are alternate congregational resources that can work better to meet those needs. Perhaps a sports program, with more focus on activity and less on social interaction, would be a more successful family environment for the Korns. Community-building for this family may mean rallying additional resources in the congregation—customizing, as it were, a place for this family to become involved and more successful—while simultaneously referring them to a more appropriate educational environment and perhaps even to parenting classes.

The bottom line is that we want to encourage all our families to try all of our programs, to be excited by our family education programs and highly motivated to participate in them, and to be successful. We don't want to give up on any family too quickly, or to give in to hasty or intolerant social pressure from other families with different ideas or styles. Nevertheless, we must pay attention to the families that seem to fail repeatedly in these settings and use our resources to find places that fit them, rather than forcing them into round holes.

Annotated Lesson Plan
(Notes for the Facilitator)

I. **CASE OVERVIEW**

- Facilitator's Summary: Clusters of eight to ten families are involved in a Jewish Family Education program that meets weekly. The educator is in charge of grouping the families. One family, the Korns, not easy to place because they are known to be difficult. The educator has received a request from one mother to exclude the Korns from her group. The educator struggles with what to do.

- Help the group determine what facts will be most useful in really understanding this case. It may be helpful to list them on the board.

II. **"WHAT IS THIS A CASE OF?"**

In the groups with which we have studied this case, participants raised issues such as:

- Balancing the social and educational components of a Jewish Family Education program
- Balancing the needs of children and the needs of parents
- Resistance to change (groups, settings)
- Educator's responsibility to please participants
- Drawing a line between education and therapy
- Matching people and programs
- Confronting the pressure to include everyone
- Dealing with difficult people (from the perspective of the leader and the other participants)
- Considerations and challenges in planning
- Knowing when to seek outside expertise or advice

Your group may come up with different or additional issues.

III. **CASE ANALYSIS**

- At this point the discussion can go in any number of directions. You may want to begin by asking the group to choose one (or more) of the issues raised above as a focus by asking them which of the issues is most relevant to their practice. Or, as a facilitator, you may want to direct the conversation by choosing one (or more) of the issues raised and directing the discussion to meet your particular agenda for the group.

- For each of your discussion foci look at how that particular situation developed.

How do the Korns themselves contribute to the situation?

What do we know about the groupings in this program?

What do we know about the educator? What is her attitude toward the program?

What is her attitude toward the Korns and other participants?

Is this a new problem?

- What did the family educator do, with what results, risks and consequences?

- How do you think the situation appeared to other participants and why do you think so?

IV. INCORPORATING THE TEXT STUDY

- How does our text study shed light on the case? (See "Large Group Discussion Point" #2.)

- Are there (other) Jewish value concepts that can help us see this issue from a Jewish perspective? See the list of "Big Jewish Ideas" in the appendix. For example: *kavod, derech eretz, klal yisrael, teshuva*—how do they apply to our situation?

V. CASE EVALUATION

- In your experience, is this situation typical?

- What might be other ways of handling this situation? What are the risks and benefits of each?

- After our discussion would you refine your idea about what this is a case of?

- What lingering questions do you have?

VI. CLOSURE—REFLECTION ON PRACTICE

Journaling and/or reflection in small groups is optional.

- Choose a question that invites participants to connect the issues raised in the case discussion to their own practice of family education. For example: Have you had to deal with difficult families in your work as a family educator? What was effective in working with them? What was not?

- Ask participants to extrapolate principles of practice—generalizations of good practice that could guide them in their own work.

- And/or have participants write about an issue from the case that was not discussed.

- And/or have participants reflect on the case study process. What new insights did you gain from our discussion? What part of the discussion did you find most challenging?

CASE # 2
JOEY

Text: The Rooster Who Would Be King

TEXT: We used Peninnah Schram's re-telling of Nachman of Bratslav's story "The Rooster Who Would be King" from her collection *Stories One Generation tells Another,* Jason Aronson, 1987

QUESTIONS FOR STUDY IN HEVRUTA

1. Peninnah Schram has called this story called "the quintessential teaching story." What do you think she meant?

2. Have you ever had to get under the table with a "rooster"? Has someone ever tried to reach you in that way? Share your story with your *hevruta.*

3. When and why does the approach of the "wise old man" work? When would you consider it **IN**appropriate?

LARGE GROUP DISCUSSION POINTS—for the facilitator

1. **The ending.** The ending of this story is potentially troubling. Is this a story about encouraging someone to stay "closeted" about his or her "true" self in order to get by in society? How else might this story be read?

2. **Teens as Roosters.** What is the relationship between the Prince and his family? At some point it says that the Prince stopped speaking the language of the King and Queen, and ultimately his connection is with someone outside his family system. Is the relationship with his parents ever healed? Can a parent be a "wise man" for his or her own child?

Case #2: Joey

As I stood by the door of the synagogue social hall greeting families as they arrived, watching them shed their jackets and hats, hang them on the hooks along the wall, greet one another and laugh, the scowl on twelve-year-old Joey Kessler's face took me by surprise. "We had to drag him," explained his father, Peter. "You know how pre-adolescents are—being with the family is a death sentence." Upon hearing his father's words, Joey deepened his scowl and hunched deeper into his jacket. His mother, Fran, shot her husband an annoyed look, turned to Joey with a smile and put her arm around him. "We always have such a good time here," she reassured him. Jennie and Jessie—the Kesslers' ten- and eight-year-olds—followed Peter, Fran and Joey into the room. As Peter, Fran, Jennie and Jessie joined the other families, talking, laughing, and helping themselves to the bagels and fruit that were spread out on the tables, Joey slouched into a nearby chair.

I was surprised and baffled by this "new" Joey. Ordinarily, during the gathering and bagel-eating part of the morning, he could be seen happily chatting and munching, or tossing a Nerf™ ball around the room with crowd of younger children in pursuit. In the two and a half years that this group of families had been involved in this program, I had always known Joey to be an enthusiastic and energetic participant. Maybe he just wasn't feeling well; maybe he had been up unusually late and had wanted to sleep in. Everyone could have an off day, even Joey. But I pondered the comment Peter had made and Fran's annoyed response as they arrived. What was that all about? "He is twelve years old," I thought. "Is he suddenly a teenager?"

The twelve families in the group included twenty adults and twenty-eight children from six to twelve. The group had been meeting monthly on Sunday mornings for Jewish text study and social action projects in a family program that these families had chosen to join as an alternative to the regular Sunday school program at their urban Reform temple. Instead of dropping their children off every Sunday, they had decided to participate in Jewish study in family context, obligating themselves to one Sunday morning per month as a large group and two additional hours a month for more Jewish learning as a family. A majority of the families had been part of the group since its inception and looked forward to these monthly Sundays. Many of the parents' social friends were part of this group, and many of the children were school friends as well.

When I called the group together on this sunny January Sunday, people took chairs or got comfortable on the rug or on the big cushions stacked in the corner, forming a jagged circle. Jennie and Jessie each settled in on a parent's lap. Joey, however, remained slouched in his chair on the periphery of the group, his scowl firmly in place. Fran tried to urge him to join the group, but he shook his head. Peter tried to jolly him out of his funk with no more success. The more formal part of the program began with singing a short version of *Birkat HaMazon*, after which I handed out study sheets for the morning's activity. The topic for that morning—Judaism and the environment—related to the upcoming holiday of *Tu Bishvat*.

Throughout the study and discussion portion of the morning I kept an eye on Joey, who looked totally bored. I was hoping that I would see a sign that he was listening.

The "action" part of the morning consisted of making birdhouses for the local nature conservancy. After our text study, which emphasized the interdependency of all living things, we talked about how the harsh winter had left the local birds and the migrating birds without their usual sources of food and shelter so that human help was needed. Everyone moved to work tables, set up with stations for building several different types of birdhouses and bird feeders. The room grew noisy with the hum of activity as people picked up wood and sandpaper, hammer and nails. The voices of people in each group reading instructions aloud and the smell of sanded wood and glue began to fill the air.

I circulated, trying to be of help as the twelve bird feeder projects got underway. Suddenly I noticed that Joey's chair was empty. Had Joey left while everyone was too busy to notice? Scanning the room, I saw Joey in the thick of the activity—hammering two pieces of wood together as Peter held them. "Sand a little faster. We're almost ready for the piece you're working on," Joey said to Jennie, and she leaned into her sanding.

"It's nice to have the old Joey back." I thought. "He seems to have pulled out of his funk. I guess when you have planned well, it works."

Two weeks went by, and I received a call from Peter, asking if he and Fran could meet with me to talk over a problem they were struggling with. We met for coffee one evening. Somewhat awkwardly, Fran and Peter told me that they had come to the decision that their family had to drop out of the Sunday morning family group. I was totally taken aback.

"It's Joey," said Fran, describing how Joey's attitude toward the group seemed to have changed overnight. (I flashed back to the scowl and the look of boredom the morning of the birdhouses.) "It's for little kids," he had said that morning. "I'm not going." I could see how this episode was causing tension as Fran described her conversation with Peter the morning of the last group gathering. "My response at the time was to try to jolly Joey out of it, while Peter felt that Joey had a point. He said Joey was almost a teenager and this is how teenagers are supposed to act and feel."

Peter picked up the narrative. "I still feel that way. This is natural. It's actually a good thing. He is supposed to be pushing away from us at this age. We should have honored that and let him stay home if that was his choice."

Fran answered, "But I've been thinking that this is a family thing and he is part of the family. I think if he can't or won't come, none of us should."

"I think this is a big mistake, Fran," added Peter. "I have seen this coming for a while with Joey. He had begun to keep himself a bit aloof from 'the kids' and made a few snide comments about being too grown up for 'this stuff.' Maybe he's right. The content might not be challenging enough." (At this last comment I felt myself beginning to feel defensive.)

"No," retorted Fran, her voice rising with emotion. "Whatever his age, he is still part of this family. Next, Jen will want to go to a friend's and Jess will have to practice piano, and we'll have no family left."

"I think you are exaggerating what this means," stated Peter.

I asked them how they felt about dropping out. They indicated that they would miss the group for their own social and intellectual stimulation, as well as for the family time together it afforded. Dropping out would also mean sending Joey, Jen and Jess to the regular Sunday school program—not the preferred option—but they were baffled by Joey's adamant refusal to come.

Joey was moving into that no-man's land of the "almost teenager." His parents were confounded—one parent seeing this as a good thing, which the family should bend to, and one seeing it as an unwelcome change that required Joey to bend to the family. There was tension between Fran and Peter, and there was sadness, too—at contemplating withdrawing from something they all had enjoyed, and at realizing that an idyllic phase of family-hood was ending as the their oldest child reached adolescence.

We all fell silent. I felt that the Kesslers were waiting for me to offer words of wisdom that would solve the puzzle. I felt a lot of weight resting on my shoulders—for this family and for "my" program; all the other families would be at this point soon. How could we manage to create a model that would work for the families, their individual members, the whole program—and me?

In my brain, I quickly sifted through what I knew about the Kesslers, teens, families with teens, my own experiences, and my own stance vis-à-vis this dilemma. Taking a deep breath, I said, "This is one of those situations in which everyone has a valid point. Joey is the oldest of the kids. He has begun to prepare for his *Bar Mitzvah*, and that is a turning point. Peter, your sense that this pulling away and assertion of maturity is natural is right on target; and Fran, your sense that family-ness is undermined if everyone just does his or her own thing is also accurate. I think the most important thing that Joey needs to know is that *we* know he's growing up. Let me try to do this by asking him to assume some additional responsibilities within the group. I'll call him myself and ask him. How does that sound?"

"It sounds like it might work," said Fran tentatively. "What kinds of things do you have in mind?" asked Peter.

I shared a few ideas with them: having Joey become the group photographer, be in charge of counting and wrapping the *tzedakah* money we collected each time, work the video camera next time we did skits, direct the next kids' production, or check the Internet for additional information for some upcoming topics. Peter and Fran both felt that all of these had some chance of working, and we parted with my promise to approach Joey.

As I drove home, I realized that, although it seemed that we had found a good (albeit experimental) approach, I was left with many lingering questions:

- Had I done an "end-run" around the problem without confronting it? One of the major challenges of parenting teens is being able to modify one's parenting style so that the teen feels recognized for his/her increasing maturity and capacity. Should I have told this to Fran and Peter explicitly, or was it enough to model it?

- Should I have just let them go? Should I have suggested that they let Joey drop out and continue to come with their other kids? Those might have been easier paths. Am I up to the challenge of keeping adolescents meaningfully involved? Maybe this just isn't a setting for adolescents.

- I was acutely aware of the differences in approach between Fran and Peter and the tension these differences seemed to create. Is this something they need help with? Is this my role? What is?

- The Kessler family is entering a new phase of the family life cycle, a phase that is exceedingly stressful in many ways, only one of which is the issue of a teen's becoming a separate individual. How in my role as family educator can I help them (and other families just behind them) cope with this phase?

- How can we help families that include teens keep teens in the family?

- Can we help families think about what their bottom-line non-negotiables are with respect to being a family—whether it is dinner time, birthdays, vacations or Jewish education?

- Is non-negotiable a useful category?

- Is there a way to help families cope with the overwhelming family-negative messages that American culture and American teen culture espouse and push? Can we offer another vision of what a family with teens can be like?

Commentary by Joel Lurie Grishaver

First words. The first issue in this case is ecological—how to construct family groups in which the ages of kids are balanced. Pre-teen and teenage kids are frequently going to have problems with being isolated if they are the only ones in their age bracket. Therefore, in the recruiting and assembling of family groups, it is important to make sure that some companionship is available for such "teens." And when groups are designed to last for years, this means looking downstream and anticipating the problem. The "companion" need not be a close friend but should be in a similar age group. In small towns, as in family gatherings where the number of peers is highly limited, there seems to be a clustering of kids based on similar age parameters. This is very much an instance of "if you can't be can't be with the one you love, love the one you are with." It is hard to be twelve and relegated to a kids' table of eight- to ten-year-olds at *seder*. There are no hard and fast rules, but eleven to twelve years old seems to be the natural boundary line in most cases. This is a pattern that family educators will face and have to accommodate. Although having only one teen in a family group will not always create difficulties, potential problems should be anticipated and can sometimes be preempted by making sure that there is another boy or girl of more or less the same age in the group. Although it is difficult to bridge the twelve- to fifteen-year-old transition, it will be easier when a number of kids, not just one, are in this age bracket.

The second issue—how to involve teens in family programs—involves the nature of adolescence in general. Somewhere between twelve and fifteen many kids pull back from family activities and seek their own paths, usually with peers, but sometimes alone. It is not only a sign of "rebellion," but also a manifestation of the need to individuate. This occurs in all kinds of arenas. Families that go to *shul* together often start to lose the participation of kids who reach this age. The same is true of many family activities, from Sunday barbecues to Friday night *shabbat* dinners. Therefore, sometimes family activities collapse as kids enter this zone. However, my experience, particularly with small towns, is that a deep sense of family/community can transcend this—even though there will be some rough moments.

It is much easier to solve problem two than problem one. In general, teens need and want a balance of family and peer group; when we can provide a balance of both, we generally do pretty well. In the model described in this case study, however, (a) Joey seems alone, isolated as a sole male twelve-year-old, and (b) no teen peer-group time is built in. In fact, being at family school seems to have isolated the pre-teens from the rest of their peers.

In this case, Joey's father states that he is acting the way "teenagers are supposed to act." The truth, however, is that Joey is acting in *one* of the ways that teenagers are prone to act. It is easy to look at a teen, or an almost teen, and say that "this is typical teen behavior." It is easier to recognize "teen behavior" than it is to predict or anticipate which of a range of behaviors a given teen or near-teen will choose. What we do know is that between eleven and eighteen, a kid has holy work to do. And that holy work has to do with re-creating a dependent child as an independent adult. The work is tough for both parent and child because it involves tearing down and reinventing a lot of relationships. That is why a twelve-year-old child can tell a mother not to touch him one moment and wind up sitting in her lap the next. It is a period filled with overreaction on both sides because overreaction is the way balance is achieved. That is why Joey was moping in a chair one moment, working with his family on the carpentry project the next, and probably back in the chair moping again in a little while.

If we are seriously interested in retaining teenagers in family education, older teens are the key to younger teens. Instead of trying to grow a family group year by year (thereby forcing one generation of kids to be the oldest each year as they turn twelve, thirteen and fourteen), we should try to form groups that are legitimately intergenerational—including sixteen- to eighteen-year-olds committed to making it work from the outset. That is a much more interesting model, because role modeling and peer leadership are built in.

Basic truths. Contrary to one implication in this case, we cannot find the "right solution" to the problem of Joey. Without knowing Joey, his family or the group, it is impossible to call the right solution, but we can suggest a range of solutions. Here are some of the things that can be tried:

1. Just wait. This may pass quickly.

2. This could be a place for the family to insist—if they can get away with "making" Joey do it. It may be a place for the family to negotiate—"do this for us and we will do *x* for you"—if they have money in the bank with the kid. Or it may fall into the category of "there are just so many fights you can fight." Only counseling with Joey and the family will tell you that. Kids are different—families are different.

3. The family educator could meet with Joey, not only to build her relationship with him, but to explore options with him. So far, the family educator's reaction to his saying "this is too babyish" has been to meet with his parents and begin a process of deciding for him. I would also wonder how much of Joey's "hostility" is stress related to being a pre-*Bar Mitzvah* and/or to moving from sixth to seventh grade.

4. Adding another family—with a similarly-aged boy—to the group would help.

5. Giving Joey a unique responsibility (like videographer) may help, though I would bet that it is successful only for a session or two. That depends on Joey's nature and on the leader's ability to notice and involve Joey, not just stick a camera in his hands.

6. Shifting the group activities so that Joey spends more time working with adults other than his parents may help a lot. That way he can see himself as one of the adults.

7. Allowing Joey to take a break from the group and involve himself in more peer-related activities for a while may be the right solution. I would not "kick" the whole family out of the family school just because it is not working for Joey at this moment, and I would make sure to decide that question with the parents. In six months or a

year Joey may be happily ready to return, especially if the invitation (not obligation) remains open. A lot depends on who misses Joey and lets him know that.

8. As a family educator, I would work hard to make sure that Joey has a Jewish peer group in place (especially since he has been pulled out of regular religious school). I would push hard on youth group, camp and future Israel plans so that the Jewish schooling stuff is being reinforced and, even if he drops out of the family school, he will move toward another motivating Jewish arena.

9. The family educator could also set up a forum in which issues of parenting Jewish adolescents could be talked about by a group of parents, including the Kesslers, outside the context of this particular family study group. Parents of younger and older kids together often can share idealism and experience in interesting ways. A person with expertise in child development and adolescent psychology can often help. This is a perfect moment for a little "Family Life Education."

10. Have some other adult in the group who has a rapport with Joey, not his parents, talk to him. This is the time for an uncle or an aunt to go where parents can't. That is part of the meaning of a "family class."

End notes. I am a little nervous about the "teacher" of this group moving into a counseling role with the family. His/her job should be to coach the family about involvement in the family class and then point them toward other experiences (or even books) that can help them deal with their issues.

My big "missing information" question in this case study is: Where are the thirteen- and fourteen-year-olds who are mentioned in the description of the group? Do they still come? Or have they withdrawn more quietly? How has the group accommodated their transition into adolescence? Or did they just escape without making a fuss? What worked in their case? And do they in some way serve as models for "Joey?" Would a call from a fourteen-year-old group member make Joey feel different? I don't know. Would the presence of sixteen- and seventeen-year-olds with their families change the dynamic? You bet. That would model the total communal age range.

If we want to learn from the village model, if we want to replicate the extended family model, it would be nice to have some grandfather in the group take a walk with Joey and offer to go fishing with him once in a while (or maybe in this day and age, to go flying with him). Such a person could ask Joey to hang in there for a while—in a way that no one else could. He could say (as he baits his hook), "After all, if I can put up with you once in a while, you could put up with a few of these young'uns once a month." (And after a great cast, he could smile at Joey, or maybe turn to him and say, "You want to try flying this plane for a while?")

Commentary by Patti Kroll

This case presents some interesting dilemmas on a number of different levels. At first glance, it seems to raise the question of how to involve family members of all ages in family programs. Upon further review, it presents additional issues of importance for family educators: not just how we can plan and implement successful family programs, but how we can meet multiple needs within a framework that is consistent with the goals of the program, as well as of the institution and those involved.

One obvious issue is how we keep teens meaningfully involved with the family, in light of the many different age groups within our programs. Some of Joey's behavior is a natural outcome of his stage of development and his evolving needs. As family educators, we need to recognize these developmental issues and find meaningful intellectual and social ways for teen family members to find value in the programs and the experience.

At a recent program for families of children in grades K-2, three of our families brought teenage siblings. These families made a decision that this was family time and, therefore, included all their children. The activities were appropriate for them to do as a family unit, yet these teens were uninterested and, at the start of the program, were wandering in the hall. While we were at somewhat of a disadvantage in not knowing in advance that they would be at the program, we made a decision as a staff to see if we could involve them in some aspect of the program. We approached them and asked if they would like to help us out. Each teen was asked to become an "expert" in one part of the art project. They could then go around to the families and assist them, as experts. Each of the teens readily agreed to this suggestion and quickly learned what they were to do. This worked successfully for the remainder of the activity. Following the program, they were thanked and told how we appreciated their help. The family educator wrote each of them a personal note thanking them for their assistance.

We learned several things from this experience. One is that it is helpful to know the ages of the children involved in advance, so that we can anticipate the needs of different age groups. Teens can be contacted prior to the program to enlist their help. In the case of Joey, this might have been a helpful proactive approach. Another thing we learned is that teens can contribute to a program and often serve as role models. They like being treated as "adults" and, as such, should be invited in an appropriate way and thanked for their help. They often have skills and interests that can add to a program. When included in this way, they are much more likely to be positive participants. The staff of this program felt that they had offered an option for these teens and were pleasantly surprised when the teens asked if they could help out at future programs.

On another level, the additional issues going on with Joey and his family raise the question of how involved a family educator should become with a family. What is our responsibility, and how far does it extend? This is a very complex issue and one that takes a great deal of professional maturity and experience. We see many kinds of families and experience many different parenting styles. In some cases we may know some of the family history, but in others we know only what we are told by the family or what we see ourselves. While we want to involve all members of our families in family programming, we do not have control of the family dynamics or the personal history they bring into our settings. This is especially true with teens, who often appear uninterested and disenfranchised from the family.

When we intervene and how much we get involved are issues that we cannot ignore. I think we do have a responsibility as professionals to assist our families, particularly when asked or when we have a concern, such as in the case with Joey. Our institutions are more than just program places. We teach and role model many different values, and we have an investment in all our children. The Kesslers have expressed some real concerns about their relationship with Joey and about parenting a teenager. The family educator is often the first person a family will turn to with a problem or concern, and I believe families look to us for guidance.

Often parents do not know what to expect at different developmental stages, and we can reaffirm that some of what they experience is normal developmental behavior. We are in a position to suggest community resources where a family can meet with other parents of teens, such as a support group through Jewish Family and Children's Services. We need to recognize our limitations, be good listeners, and know when we are in over our heads and can guide a family to a place where they can get the support they need.

It is evident that the Kesslers have different parenting styles and ways of responding to Joey. As professionals, we are in a position to model positive ways to interact, and we often have greater success approaching a child than the parents. Generally, I go directly to teens to ask them to help out. I always give them the option of refusing or ask for their suggestions of what might work. To avoid conflict with the parents, the teens and I agree what we will tell or ask their parents and who will contact them. I believe it is critical for teens to trust the adults they come into contact with and to feel we honestly care about them.

Another issue raised in this case is how we keep our teens involved in synagogue programming. Studies show that the most critical time for identity development is during the teen years, yet that is the time when our teens pull away from their parents and from the synagogue. These are the kids we want and need. We fear losing them. Our task is to find multiple ways for them to continue their involvement in our programs, including family programs. There are several things we can do to make this happen. Teens like to feel some control over situations and may often need a reason to be involved. This is why I might enlist their help planning a program or taking on specific responsibilities. The suggestions that Joey be the photographer or take charge of tzedakah are good places to begin.

There is more to it than that, however, because it is important to meet with the individual teen and find out what his or her interests are. Is photography an area he would like to take on? If not, might he like to contribute to the program? We have had great success with teen assistants in our classrooms and find that, when given responsibility and held accountable, they understand the importance of their role and often view involvement in the synagogue differently. When they are helping out in a class or at a program, they are listening and learning. These are the times when we can provide positive reinforcement, such as praise for something they have done, or talking about their ease with children or their leadership with a particular project. A little bit of praise goes a long way with teens and works much better coming from an adult other than the parent.

The case of Joey asks what defines family and how that changes from time to time and from situation to situation. When a group of families has been together for programming, as this group has been, the loss of one family is felt by the entire group and can weaken the social structure. This is more than a group of families who get together once a month. It is a group in which both the adults and the children have formed friendships with other families. It has offered an alternative way of learning for the entire family, one that has been successful and has kept the families involved in study within and outside the synagogue.

When the Kesslers indicated they were going to pull out of the group, I wondered if that was a family decision or a parent decision. I am a believer in family meetings to work out issues that affect the entire family and to look for possible solutions. There is more to this family than just Joey and his parents. There are two younger siblings who are taking notes on everything that is going on. A decision to pull out of the group would affect them as well, and we want family units to listen to all who are involved. The whole family has a dilemma. The children may be able to come up with suggestions that the parents never thought of.

One question Joey's family (and all families) can and should ask is "What is negotiable?'" What are the core values of this family and what are we willing to compromise? Articulating personal and family values so that children understand them provides a framework for what is meaningful to their family, what it means for them to be a family, and it guides family decision-making. Many families create "Family Mission Statements." This work might be done at Rosh Hashanah and revised each year. That is the time when families talk about what they want to accomplish in the coming year, including family vacations, extracurricular activities, personal goals, their Jewish family life and their continuing involvement Jewish family programs. In this way, each family member has the opportunity to share thoughts and ideas as to what it means for them to be a family.

These are very tough issues that confront us every day. I believe they require patience, understanding and thoughtful reflection about the people involved, our goals and values. They also require us to understand that we cannot meet with success in every situation. Every family, every child, every soul is precious. It pains us to lose one family or one child. Our efforts are directed toward finding ways to keep each person involved in Jewish life and remembering always that to save one person is to have saved the entire world.

Annotated Lesson Plan
(Notes for the Facilitator)

I. **CASE OVERVIEW**

- *Facilitator's Summary:* Twelve-year-old Joey no longer wishes to participate with his family in a monthly family education program that is an alternative to religious school at their temple. His parents meet with the educator to discuss the situation. The educator is left with many lingering questions about her role, the future of her program, working with families with teens and helping families set boundaries for themselves.

- *Help the group determine what facts will be most useful in really understanding this case. It may be helpful to list them on the board.*

II. **"WHAT IS THIS A CASE OF?"**

In the groups with which we have studied this case, participants raised issues such as:

- Balancing the needs of different members of a group/family
- Helping a family in transition
- Defining the boundaries of family education—whom is it for?
- Challenges of an ongoing program, the life span of a program
- A challenging participant
- Drawing the line between therapy and education
- "Intervening" in parenting issues
- Adolescents in family education settings

Your group may come up with different or additional issues.

III. **CASE ANALYSIS**

- *At this point the discussion can go in any number of directions. You may want to begin by asking the group to choose one (or more) of the issues raised above as a focus by asking them which of the issues is most relevant to their practice. Or, as a facilitator, you may want to direct the conversation by choosing one (or more) of the issues raised and directing the discussion to meet your particular agenda for the group.*

- *For each of your discussion foci look at how that particular situation developed.*

    How do the players themselves (Joey, his parents, the writer) contribute to the situation?

    What do we know about the program?

    What do we know about the educator? What is her attitude toward the program? What is her attitude toward Joey, his family and other participants?

    Is this a new problem?

- *What did the family educator do, with what results, risks and consequences?*
- *How do you think the situation appeared to other participants and why do you think so?*

IV. INCORPORATING THE TEXT STUDY

- *How does our text study shed light on the case? (See "Large Group Discussion Point"#2.)*
- *Are there (other) Jewish value concepts that can help us see this issue from a Jewish perspective? See the list of "Big Jewish Ideas" in the appendix. For example: kavod, sh'lom bayit, derech eretz–how do they apply to our situation?*

V. CASE EVALUATION

- *In your experience, is this situation typical?*
- *What might be other ways of handling this situation? What are the risks and benefits of each?*
- *After our discussion would you refine your idea about what this is a case of?*
- *What lingering questions do you have?*

VI. CLOSURE–REFLECTION ON PRACTICE

Journaling and/or reflection in small groups is optional.

- *Choose a question that invites participants to connect the issues raised in the case discussion to their own practice of family education.*

  For example: Have you ever been asked for parenting advice from program participants? Where are your boundaries–when do you offer advice and when do you refer them to others?

- *Ask participants to extrapolate principles of practice–generalizations of good practice that could guide them in their own work.*
- *And/or have participants write about an issue from the case that was not discussed.*
- *And/or have participants reflect on the case study process: What new insights did you gain from our discussion? What part of the discussion did you find most challenging?*

CASE #3
DAZE OF AWE

Text: Rav Rahumi

TEXT: The Babylonian Talmud, Ketubot 62b (Aramaic & English translation)

CONTEXT: Note that it was customary for scholars to study all year at the academy and return to their families only periodically (like modern boarding schools). Also, it is important to realize that in that time the meal before Yom Kippur was a very big deal (it had the kind of importance as a family time as the Passover seder or Thanksgiving supper does for us today). It was also a time when one asked forgiveness from people, as Yom Kippur does not offer atonement for that. (Yom Kippur offers atonement only for sins committed against God.) By not going home Rav Rahumi has not been able to approach the holiday having been forgiven by his wife. Finally, it seems from the text that Rav Rahumi and his wife would never have children as the only night he was home (erev Yom Kippur) was a night when sexual relations are prohibited.

QUESTIONS FOR STUDY IN HEVRUTA

1. How would you title this story?

2. In Aramaic (the original language of this version of the story), Rabbi Rahumi's name means Rabbi "Lover" or Rabbi "Loving." How do you understand his name in the context of the story?

3. What is the significance of the timing of the story to coincide with Erev Yom Kippur?

4. Why did the roof collapse?

5. What happened next?

6. Can you identify with any of the characters in the story? In what ways?

LARGE GROUP DISCUSSION POINT—for the facilitator

Being self-critical: On one level this story is a story about rabbis criticizing themselves. Rav Rahumi is studying with the best teacher at a very important school. This would lead the reader to imagine that Rav Rahumi is going to be presented as an ideal student, and yet when the house of study collapses underneath him we are brought to understand that not only is his behavior being condemned but also that of his teachers and his school. The foundation upon which he rests is literally and symbolically empty. As teachers, when we look at a story like this and see the extreme imbalance in Rav Rahumi's life we are asked to critique our own work habits and the effect they have on our health (spiritual and physical) and the health of those close to us.

Text Study

Breishit Raba 95 (manuscript)

1. Rabbi Rahumi was studying with Rava [a great teacher] in Mahuza [the site of an important school]

   and it was customary for him to return home every "erev" [the day before] Yom Kippur

2. One day he was drawn into his studies [lit. "the law"]

3. His wife was expecting him.

4. He's coming now. He's coming now…

5. He did not come.

6. She became deeply depressed [lit. "her mind was weakened].

7. A tear fell from her eye.

8. He was sitting on the roof [of the school].

9. The roof collapsed under him and he died [lit "his soul rested].

1. כי הא דרב רחומי היה
   שכיח קמיה דרבא במחוזא
   הוה רגיל דהוה אתי
   לביתי הכל מילי יומא
   דכיפורי

2. יומא חד משכתיה שמעתא

3. היה מסכיא דביתהן

4. השתא אתי השתא אתי

5. לא אתא,

6. חלש דעתה

7. אחית דמעתא מענה

8. הוה יתיב באיגרא

9. אפחית איגרא מתותיה
   זנה נפשיה

Case #3: Daze of Awe

The Days of Awe are approaching. It is time to plan, prepare and focus on the Family High Holiday services for Rosh Hashanah and Yom Kippur. As a Jewish family educator, I look forward to the preparation and planning of these two one-and-a-half-hour-long services. As a parent and wife, I find this time of the year overwhelming. I feel I must do a juggling act with my domestic life and my professional life.

Suzie, our cantor, and I have been co-leading these services for over five years. I also receive a small stipend for this position each year. The planning begins in the spring prior to the High Holidays. The planning continues over the summer in two-hour sessions, sitting by the pool with our kids or at the park, discussing the details and the different ways we want to involve families, children and religious school classes in the services. We work hard to develop a schedule for each family service so that it dovetails with the timeline of the main congregational service. Timing is carefully worked out with the rabbi and the High Holiday planning committee so that people can attend the Shofar service in the main service for Rosh Hashanah and to hear the rabbi's sermon on Yom Kippur.

About three weeks before the holidays begin we are ready to rehearse, making sure we have the *t'fillot* down, choreographing our steps on the *bima* and so on, until we have a basic feel for the flow of the service we have worked so hard to create. We have our final meeting with the rabbi to check over what we have planned, and another meeting with the High Holiday planning committee to make sure all the logistics are taken care of.

Just when we think we are set, the tension begins. We have to think about our own families. We must clean the house, prepare the holiday meals and decide if we can handle making a big family dinner that includes the *bubies, zadies,* aunts, uncles and cousins. At this point I become exhausted just thinking about all the preparation involved and simply want a small, intimate dinner with my husband and children. Of course, this is bound to upset my children because they look forward to those big family dinners. I hope that by now I have created a picture of the stress and sacrifice that has to be made in my own family's High Holiday experience.

Last year a particularly upsetting incident occurred at one of our Family High Holiday services that illustrates this dilemma. Actually, the Rosh Hashanah family service was going really well. There must have been over three hundred people in attendance. Families were participating with English readings, ark openings, and so on. The seventh-grade *Bat/Bar Mitzvah* class took a wonderful leadership role in the Torah service. After completing the Torah service, Suzie and I were marveling at the different levels of participation.

Then it happened! While we were standing on the *bima*, a sense of loss combined with embarrassment hit both of us at the same time. We saw our five-year-old children running in the back of the sanctuary; our fifteen- and twelve-year-olds, who had been sitting in the front pew, were no longer there. What happened? We saw other families sitting with their children. Did our children feel left out, neglected or forgotten? We had asked the older children to sit next to the younger ones because our spouses were attending the main service. Why did the older ones leave, and why were the younger ones running around? We simply did not know.

As a Jewish family educator, I often wonder how my job affects my own family's Jewish experience. Must I expect my children to be perfect models? I often wonder if I will resent this sacrifice—of depriving my own family of High Holiday togetherness because of my leadership role. I have also tried to think of ways to include my own children in the service so they have an opportunity to be with me for a brief moment up on the *bima*. These are just some of the dilemmas we must face in taking on a leadership role.

Commentary by Shellie Dickstein

SD, family educator for a central educational agency, agreed to write a commentary to illuminate a case study on family education. She is expected to complete the task in three months but is not sure how she will do so, since she must attend to it during non-work hours when her children make demands, holidays intercede, an unplanned conference calls her away for several days, and her family has taken to leaving her messages in the layers of dust accumulating on the furniture. Each time she thinks about putting fingers to keyboard at home, her palms become sweaty and her heart is racing, because the case so clearly speaks to the anxiety she herself experiences whenever she struggles to balance her professional and personal lives. What makes this all the more difficult is precisely the perceived lack of boundaries between the Jewish work she does as a family educator and the Jewish life she leads as a family member. Wait a minute! She has a moment of clarity. Maybe this could actually be a good thing. Maybe this last thought will be helpful in revealing a lens through which to look at these issues.

One of the important goals of Jewish family education is enabling families to become better families. By creating better Jewish families—through new Jewish knowledge, skills and modes of learning—we strengthen the family itself. When families set aside time for Jewish learning they share ideas, learn to communicate and intensify their respect for each other. When families create their own Jewish experiences they build collective memories, reaffirm their values and reflect on what they contribute to each other. Family education gives them opportunities to think about what kind of a family they are and what kind of a family they might become. These are the very same questions that we, with our own families and with the congregational families, need to keep in mind and discuss from the very start of the family education process. The more we encourage families to be part of this process, the more we help families work better as families. In addition, the way we perceive our leadership role and style, vis-à-vis the families we work with, impacts both how much they are empowered and the positive or negative effects our work has on our own family.

Family education and systems theory. A systems approach, particularly family systems theory, can help us think differently about our role as family educators and help us "create different strategies for inducing change."[1] Family systems theory can be applied to organizational systems such as the synagogue, and to the role of the family educator in the system. In this commentary I will use family systems theory to illuminate some of the obvious and not-so-obvious issues raised in this case: the negative impact our work can have on our family life, burnout and an overfunctioning leadership style. I am grateful to a modern commentator, Rabbi Edwin H. Friedman, whose groundbreaking work, *Generation to Generation: Family Process in Church and Synagogue*, clarifies the role of the

---

[1] Edwin Friedman, *Generation to Generation: Family Process in Church and Synagogue*, The Guilford Press (New York and London), 1986, p. 17

clergy in the synagogue system. His work, by extension, helped me to better understand the role of the family educator, her relationship with the families in her programs and the impact of the profession on her own family. Friedman writes:

> These too are families (synagogues). They function as organic structures in their own right, according to the rules and models of family life...But religious institutions not only function like families, they also contain families. Indeed, they often derive their very structure from families. Thus, emotional process in religious organizations not only mirrors emotional process in personal families, but also both types of family systems plug into one another. That is a major reason why unresolved issues in any of the clergy's three families (family of birth, his/her present family, and the synagogue family) can produce symptoms in one of the others, and why within that emotional interlock often lies the key to knowledge or to further stress.[2]

Family systems theory teaches that each member of a system or organization impacts all the other members as well as the system itself. According to Friedman, "Family theory can be applied to all work systems, depending primarily on 1) the degree of emotional interdependence in that relationship system, and 2) *the extent to which its business is 'life.'*"[3] By these criteria, family theory is highly applicable to family education. First, our concern for the families we work with, and our emotional link to them—because we see ourselves as role models—contributes to emotional interdependence. Second, the business of family education is "life"—the gut-wrenching, emotionally charged aspects of life: life cycle events, spirituality, values and relationships. As family educators we often think of the families we work with as members of a system, and we are concerned with how they function during and after the family education program. Rarely, however, do we try to understand our place as an integral part of this system. Even though we understand that the boundaries between our Jewish work and our Jewish lives are blurred, we rarely analyze the significance of this problem until it is too late. As Friedman teaches, "There is an intrinsic relationship between our capacity to put families together and our ability to put ourselves together."[4]

Overfunctioning family educators. One of the givens about family educators is that their work is labor-intensive and emotionally involving. There are so many variables to consider, details to work out and personalities to deal with; planning and executing even one event takes an enormous amount of time and energy. While we often want others to share the load, we find it difficult to encourage our members to take responsibility for the tasks that are vital to supporting the program or for their own learning and Jewish practice. This is partially because our existing systems encourage us to become "overfunctioning" leaders—shouldering the responsibility for everything. As Friedman recognizes:

---

[2]*Ibid.*, p. 195 [3]*Ibid.*, p. 197 [4]*Ibid.*, p. 3

> One of the most universal complaints from clergy of all faiths is the feeling of being stuck with all the responsibility….All this focus on getting the other to take responsibility has a 'familiar' ring. It echoes the sound of parents or spouses caught in an overfunctioning position in their families….What rarely occurs to those in the overfunctioning position is that in any type of family the rest of the system may be underfunctioning as an adaptive response! In other words, it has become a familial, homeostatic correction (the need for the system to maintain its state of balance), to an extreme position. No one remembers the overfunctioner's birthday; he or she is less likely to be forgiven for mistakes. Overfunctioning in any system is an anxious response in both senses of the word, 'anxious' as in anticipatory and 'anxious' as in 'fearful'….*One of the subtlest yet most fundamental effects of overfunctioning is spiritual. It destroys the spiritual quality of the overfunctioner. Several ministers and rabbis have reported, after switching professions: 'Now I can go back to being a good Christian/Jew; now I can enjoy prayers and the Holy Days again.'* [5]

These ideas, which are well illustrated in this case, have profound implications for our roles of leaders. Overfunctioning leaves us feeling vulnerable to the slightest criticism and fearful about our image (especially when our own children at a family education event are not behaving as we would like). It also takes away from our ability to enjoy, on a personal level, the holiday or ritual in which we are involved.

Burnout

> A family model of burnout asks what are the characteristics of a congregational family emotional system most likely to burn out its spiritual leader or promote symptoms in his or her nuclear family….[one of these] is the extent to which the leadership allows the congregation[al work] to pre-empt its entire emotional life [no other friends or social networks].[6]

We often see our role as motivators who, according to Friedman,

> function as though their followers did not know what is good for them and, furthermore, would never change were it not for their efforts. Teachers, salesmen and therapists also tend to think this way. In addition, leaders tend to assume that if they have failed to change the heads of their followers, it is because they, the leaders, did not try hard enough.[7]

Perhaps there is an alternative model for seeing our roles as part of the system. Instead of planning everything *for* families, we could plan *with* families. That would enable the

---

[5]*Ibid.*, pp. 211-212 [6]*Ibid.*, p. 217 [7]*Ibid.*, p. 223 [8]*Ibid.*, p. 228 [9]*Ibid.*, p. 226

families we work with to take more responsibility, empowering them and enabling us to have more time to enjoy our own families, particularly at busy holiday times. Stepping back and relinquishing some control is not easy and requires that we conceptualize our role very differently.

Leadership styles. According to Friedman, there are three paradigms of leadership: the charismatic approach, the consensus approach and, last but most healthy, the "self-differentiation" approach—"the ability of a leader to be a self while still remaining part of the system...keeping in mind that successful leadership means not only moving a family toward its goals but also maximizing its functioning, as well as the health and survival of both the family and its leader." [8]

Where does the charismatic approach fall short?

Leadership by charisma has difficulty with succession. Families or historical movements that become too dependent on their leaders tend to lose their purpose after the loss of such leaders. [Also] leadership by charisma ultimately is not healthy for the leader. He or she is perpetually forced to overfunction....For these reasons, and more, the charismatic leader remains in a chronic state of stress. [9]

And what of the consensus approach?

> The basic emphasis in the consensus approach is on the will of the group...being more concerned with the development of a cohesive infrastructure. It tends to value peace over progress and personal relationships (feelings) over ideas. It abhors polarization. Since the will of the group is supposed to develop out of its own personality, rather than come down from the top, the function of the leader becomes more of a resource person or an *enabler*. The family led by consensus will tend to be less imaginative...Leaderless groups are more easily panicked and the anxiety tends to escalate....Emphasis on consensus gives strength to the extremists. [10]

In contrast, a self-differentiated person can define her role as leader, set goals and maintain a strong connection to the group without being engulfed by it:

> Leadership through self-differentiation does not create polarity between the leader and the follower. Instead, the family systems concept of leadership looks at how they function as *part* of one another. If a leader will take primary responsibility for his or her own position as 'head' and work to define his or her own goals and self, *while staying in touch* with the rest of the organism, there is more than a reasonable chance that the body will follow. Leadership through self-differentiation turns the table on dependency. As long as the leader is trying to change his or her followers, the latter are in the 'cat-bird's' seat. As long as the head, or the rest of the body, makes its functioning dependent on the other's functioning, the organism is in control. But when the leader is concentrating on where he or she is

[10]*Ibid.*, p. 27   [11]*Ibid.*, p. 229

'headed,' the effects of that dependency are reversed. It is the dependents who now feel the pressure. The ball is in their court.[11]

As leaders, we must work toward defining our *own goals* and preserving *the self*. As family educators, we must take our own needs and the needs of our own families into consideration along with the needs of the families with whom we work. We can plan for and discuss with our congregational families the family issues they encounter when joining family education events and the impact this has on our own families.

Brainstorming with families. My colleague and friend, Janet Zimmerman (MSW, CSW and the past chair of the Family Life Education Committee of her own synagogue), suggested that we explore with our own family and our congregational families—by brainstorming or discussion—the effects a family education event may have on each member of the family. What does it feel like to be the child in the sanctuary whose parent is on the *bima*? How might congregational families react to our own children? How do the fathers feel—both those who are coming to the family education event and our own husbands who may have to share responsibilities while we are working? How do we feel when preparing for a family education event saps us of our energy and ability to enjoy our own celebration?

In exploring such questions, the first step is understanding the feelings of all family members, thereby sensitizing ourselves and gaining perspective. Then we can brainstorm creative solutions. Perhaps after sharing our feelings with our own families, we could create new holiday rituals that allow us to spend alternative time with our husbands and children to compensate for time "lost" when our work demands that we be apart from them for the traditional holiday services or rituals. Perhaps we will discover sources of support for our own children in other families or older members of the congregation. Input from our congregational families might lead us to change the structure or timing of the service or event to be more flexible, or to share responsibility for planning and leading services with other participants in the family program, which would create greater ownership and less polarity. Discussing with our children and husband how the upcoming event will affect them and us will give them the opportunity to shoulder some responsibility for creative solutions. Seeing ourselves as part of the system equalizes the responsibility of all family members, creates stronger families and makes the system work better for everyone. In this way we might truly reap the benefits of working as a family, with families and as family educators.

After returning from the educational conference, SD felt very anxious. Not only did she have to catch up on work at her agency, she needed to complete the case commentary and spend much-needed time with her family. Trying to pull at least two of these elements together, one Sunday she enlisted her husband's guidance and insight on the case (thank you, PD!). They decided to work at his office in a school building, where their children could play in the gym and on the stage in the auditorium. They took breaks to play basketball together as a family. This much-needed support and peace of mind enabled SD to complete her task.

Commentary by Joan Wolchansky

This case study illuminates some basic truths about family education:
- Often the same people lead family education programs year after year;
- Home family celebrations are as important as congregational celebrations to families;
- Not all family members understand the importance of family education in and of itself;
- There are no perfect models of family education and no perfect children; and
- Working in one's own congregation presents unique challenges.

For each of these basic truths there is at least one alternative way of thinking about the issues. For example, one way of dealing with having the same people leading family education programs year after year—here, the family educator and the cantor—might lie in the planning process. In this case, the congregation has a High Holiday planning committee, out of which could come a High Holiday family service subcommittee. That subcommittee could be helpful in sharing some of the responsibilities of the family educator and the cantor so that while they remain the main facilitators of the service, they are not the only ones planning and leading it.

Although committees often create extra work, they can make our jobs easier in the long run. Additionally, one of our goals as family educators is empowering families to learn and feel comfortable about their own Judaic family practices, knowledge, beliefs and values. What better way to empower them than to involve them in planning and implementing the family service—a learning process in and of itself. While the family educator's and cantor's summer sessions at the park and pool sound delightful, they limit the possibilities of involving other congregational professionals and lay leaders in the planning process and their access to material resources that might be needed during that process. Further, with more people having a greater investment in the service, the family educator might have more time to relate to her own family, both before the holidays and during the service itself.

Sharing the responsibility with others also enables us to "think outside the box" when it comes to programs that have been successful and do not necessarily need retooling. The family educator has had a successful service in the past and enjoys the planning and preparation, so there was not necessarily a compelling need to rethink it. Rethinking how the service is conducted, however, could provide the family educator and cantor with an opportunity to brainstorm with their own children as to their roles in the service while their mothers led the service. One possibility that might have emerged from such brainstorming, for example, would be having the family educator sit with the two sets of children for a part of the service and the cantor sit with the children for another part.

Because we tend to characterize what happens in the home as personal and what happens outside the home (in the congregation) as work-related, our own families might not understand the importance of family education for themselves. We are lucky in that, unlike workers in many other professions, we *do* have an opportunity to involve our families in our work. While a doctor would not bring her child into the operating room to perform surgery, and a lawyer cannot ask her child to try a case in court, family educators can involve their children and spouses in their work, so they become program participants themselves. Our older children can participate as *madrichim* (counselors) and thereby provide us with another source of manpower. Younger children can participate actively in the program itself. It is critical to enlist the help of the spouses as program participants as well. They will then feel invested in the program and can also parent the children while the family educator is working.

If the importance of being together as a family is processed with our spouses and children in advance, they might develop a sense of ownership in the service instead of seeing it as just another work situation. The more understanding families have of what we do, the more willing they may be to be cooperative participants. They may also feel more involved in the family decision-making process. In this case I was struck by the fact that the leaders' spouses attended the main service. This might have sent a subtle message that that they didn't think that the family service was as important, meaningful, spiritual, etc. as the main service.

Another way of thinking outside the box in this case would be to look at the actual structure of the family service (and, by extension, other family education programs). Why do family education programs need to mimic traditional programs, i.e., have leaders up on the *bima*, etc.? If there are no perfect models of family education and no one definitive way of doing things, we are free to try alternative models of programming. While we do not want our children running around the room, we can allow flexibility in the physical set-ups, innovative formats for services, etc. In a sense, by virtue of being family educators, we have license to free ourselves from replicating other programs and to create new approaches.

Working in one's own congregation presents interesting challenges. On the one hand, we can all readily describe the downside. It is difficult to separate our professional role from our congregant/member role, especially when we are constantly approached by congregants with questions and complaints during non-working hours (particularly on *shabbatot* and holidays when we are not providing a family education program). If we have work-related issues, our congregation—which is supposed to be a safe place to replenish our souls—is no longer a safe haven. We also see all the warts that one sees whenever one gets involved in an organization; we may learn too much about what *really* goes on in the congregation. Finally, congregations often lack formalized human resources policies and professional supervision, so that their work environments may be less professional than those in other organizations.

On the other hand, there are many benefits to working in one's own congregation that are compelling in and of themselves. We feel we are connected and part of a family, not just employees. We develop a sense of ownership about congregational programs, and we have the opportunity to develop meaningful relationships with our congregant-clients. We know the network and culture of the congregation, and that knowledge provides a comfort level with the workplace. Because of this, we can hit the ground running when we first start our jobs; the learning curve is taken care of. In our own congregation, we can have some flexibility in our work schedule. We share the denominational ideology of the congregation, so we identify with the goals and objectives. Finally, working in our own congregation gives us an identity and niche, which otherwise can be hard to achieve, especially in larger congregations.

This case also illustrates the dilemma that we all face as professional Jewish family educators: that of juggling our professional and personal lives so that our own Jewish family lives remain at the top of our own agendas. Achieving that correct balance is probably one of the hardest things we have to do. As seen in this case, often by the time that a Jewish holiday comes around, we have been so busy preparing for everyone else that we are exhausted at the prospect of preparing for our own family's celebration. Our dual role also means that we have to do double planning—for our own family's celebration and for that of our professional constituents.

We must allow ourselves to make the most of the time that we do have with our families. Even if we have a less-than-ideal *shabbat* because we have been getting ready for a big *shabbat* program in our job, even if we put up our own *sukkah* at the last minute because we have been involved in a *Sukkot* family education program, our own *shabbat* and *sukkah*-building are just as meaningful to our families.

In addition to making the most of whatever moments we do have, there are concrete ways that we can help our own family life flourish. We can take advantage of the times when we do not have deadlines or major programs to spend special separate time with each child and spouse. We can work on a special project, such as creating a memory scrapbook together, or go on a special outing with each child alone. We can cook a favorite meal or play a neglected board game. We can establish a Family Movie Night once a month, with favorite videos, popcorn and pizza.

Since we are outward-oriented, we often forget that our own families enjoy the materials we create and use in our jobs. We are lucky to have immediate access to a wealth of wonderful Jewish family education materials, such as games, videos, cassettes and books, that we can share with our own families first. We can involve our families in helping to create *shabbat* and holiday atmospheres in our homes—by cooking with us, setting the table, or just requesting a special food. If we can maintain a sense of fun, humor, joy and excitement, and not look at our interactions with our own families as "mini-family education programs," our families can benefit tremendously from our organizational skills and multitude of resources.

The reality is that we have a double whammy: We are both working parents and professional Jews who don't want to turn our own families off to being Jewish. Ultimately, however, I think that the most special thing that we can do for our families is to model behaviors and Jewish values by virtue of the profession we have chosen, and hope that our families, particularly our children, will learn to value *that* as they grow up. In the long run, if we can juggle our personal and professional lives, both our home and work situations can be enriched.

Annotated Lesson Plan
(Notes for the Facilitator)

I. **CASE OVERVIEW**

- *Facilitator's Summary:* The cantor and educator co-lead Family High Holiday services at their synagogue. After intense preparation for their professional roles they contend with their own families' experience of the holidays. The educator struggles with the stresses that her professional role places on her own family.

- *Help the group determine what facts will be most useful in really understanding this case. It may be helpful to list them on the board.*

II. **"WHAT IS THIS A CASE OF?"**

In the groups with which we have studied this case, participants raised issues such as:

- Balancing personal and professional obligations
- The dilemmas posed for the family of a Jewish community professional
- Role modeling
- Seeking spiritual satisfaction for oneself while helping others attain theirs
- The challenges of planning
- The vulnerability of the professional

Your group may come up with different or additional issues.

III. **CASE ANALYSIS**

- *At this point the discussion can go in any number of directions. You may want to begin by asking the group to choose one (or more) of the issues raised above as a focus by asking them which of the issues is most relevant to their practice. Or, as a facilitator, you may want to direct the conversation by choosing one (or more) of the issues raised and directing the discussion to meet your particular agenda for the group.*

- *For each of your discussion foci look at how that particular situation developed.*

  How do the players themselves (the Cantor and the writer) contribute to the situation?

  What do we know about the educator and her family?

  What is her attitude toward the program?

  Is this a new problem?

- *What did the family educator do, with what results, risks and consequences?*

- *How do you think the situation appeared to other participants and why do you think so?*

IV. INCORPORATING THE TEXT STUDY

- *How does our text study shed light on the case? (See "Large Group Discussion Point" 1.)*
- *Are there (other) Jewish value concepts that can help us see this issue from a Jewish perspective? See the list of "Big Jewish Ideas" in the appendix. For example: kavvana, sh'lom bayit, tefilla–how do they apply to our situation?*

V. CASE EVALUATION

- *In your experience, is this situation typical?*
- *What might be other ways of handling this situation? What are the risks and benefits of each?*
- *After our discussion would you refine your idea about what this is a case of?*
- *What lingering questions do you have?*

VI. CLOSURE–REFLECTION ON PRACTICE

Journaling and/or reflection in small groups is optional.

- *Choose a question that invites participants to connect the issues raised in the case discussion to their own practice of family education.*

   For example: How does your professional role affect your personal/family life? How do you handle the tension between the two?

- *Ask participants to extrapolate principles of practice–generalizations of good practice that could guide them in their own work.*
- *And/or have participants write about an issue from the case that was not discussed.*
- *And/or have participants reflect on the case study process: What new insights did you gain from our discussion? What part of the discussion did you find most challenging?*

CASE # 4
ROAD BLOCK

Text: Yitro's Advice

TEXT: Exodus 18:13-27 (Hebrew & English translation)

CONTEXT: Yitro (Jethro), Moses's father-in-law, himself a Midianite priest, criticizes Moses's inefficient procedure for judging the people. Yitro advises Moses to delegate and proposes organizing a judicial system.

QUESTIONS FOR STUDY IN HEVRUTA

1) What is the basis of Yitro's concern?

2) How would you characterize Yitro's behavior toward Moses and his tone in addressing Moses?

3) What are the necessary conditions for Moses to delegate responsibility?

4) What conditions are necessary for you to feel comfortable delegating responsibility to other staff, to parents and to children?

LARGE GROUP DISCUSSION POINT—for the facilitator

"They Just Don't Get It"—One of the problems with delegating is trusting the other person to understand your goals and heed your vision. How do you communicate your vision and your goals? What do you do when the other person just doesn't get it?

Case #4: Road Block

I asked Dan, the school director, how the plans for the *b'nai mitzvah* ropes course program were evolving. "We gave the parents the option of attending," he replied casually. He explained that the school can't require them to attend, especially since it doesn't really have the money for the $60 adult fee and can afford to subsidize only the students.

I felt my "but then it's not family education" alarm going off. The ropes course, an Outward Bound-type experience, had originally become part of the seventh-grade family curriculum years before, when I worked quarter-time in the congregation as the family educator. I believed the program was a good example of family education for families with teens, and I was proud of having created such a successful program. The experience of parents and teens taking new risks and challenges together (and seeing the rabbi jump out of a tree) lent itself to a family program on coming-of-age issues that arise during the *bar/bat mitzvah* year. We had combined the outdoor component with a text study session and a follow-up program.

Dan may not have been aware that the "family" part of the program had lost its soul. He was less familiar than I with family education. But the problems weren't limited to just this program; they extended to all the other family programs throughout the congregation.

Now, seven years after the inception of family education at our synagogue—a congregation of 300 households—membership was stable but not thriving. Financial and people resources were scarce, especially after the congregation made the large financial commitment of hiring a full-time professional educational director for the religious school—a decision that was long overdue. While Dan was vocally supportive of family education, he didn't seem to understand what it really meant. He often spoke of it as "parent involvement." While Dan talked about the need to get parents out of their cars and into the school, to him this often meant having *shabbat* grade-level dinners, a concert for families to attend together, or parents' volunteering at the religious school. He seemed to view family education as just one part of the educational program, one that competed with other priorities. During Dan's first two years at the congregation, he and I met regularly with the rabbi, and Dan participated in seminars sponsored by the Bureau of Jewish Education-based Jewish Family Education Project. But when it came down to implementing programs, the actual family piece was weak, absent or tacked on last minute. (Trained many years earlier at a strong program for reform educators, Dan did keep current on developments in the field of Jewish education and attended national conferences as well as local professional development programs.)

The family education department, which I began in 1991, had a strong and successful history. Efforts by the synagogue board to strengthen the program had succeeded in forming a lay committee that included a supportive board member and experienced staff representatives. Nevertheless, I constantly felt that I had to "sell" the program and remind people what family education was and was not. In addition, it still took a great deal of publicity and many phone calls and reminders by me to get people to family events, and the execution of most programs was exhausting.

The rabbi boosted family education in the boardroom and from the pulpit as the program of the entire congregation. He would say, "Our effort to offer family education to the whole congregation, not just to the school, has included events of varying size and scope with diverse target audiences." The rabbi and I shared a broad vision of family education as including singles to seniors, young couples expecting their first child to parents who have already launched their kids into college and the workplace. Somehow, however, we had failed to sell this inclusive vision to our constituents.

Despite winning awards and grants in the community, I am still the one who "pushes" our family education department forward. Family education is too highly identified with one person—me. The program is still not deeply rooted in the synagogue. Looking back, it seems to me that most participants/congregants felt that this was "the rabbi and family educator show"—the successful work of two individuals. Furthermore, to many congregants family still means kids and kids means school.

It was difficult to fit my own vision of family education to the confines of my limited paid position. I wanted the lay committee members to engage in time-consuming politicking to boost community support. I wanted a family education insert in the bulletin four times a year. I wanted fewer extravaganza-style events and more ongoing programs that included a strong study element. I wanted a committee that called *me*. I wanted a job description that I didn't write! I wanted a desk and a place to work!

Was I suffering from a bad case of burnout? Was it impossible to be both a congregant and an employee? Was it simply time for me to move on and let go, even if it meant the end of the program I had started?

Commentary by Esther Netter

At first glance, the story as presented by the author of this case seems illogical and curious. She invented a new family education program, watched it grow and achieve community recognition, and then saw it shrink. At second glance, this case raises many familiar issues.

The first issue is how a Jewish family education program becomes deep-rooted in a community. How much do we think about the process of establishing a family education program? Any new program will take time to deep-root in an institution. That process requires both short-term and long-term planning at the outset. Before proceeding, look at other programs in this synagogue. Which projects succeeded, and which have failed, over the years? What variables made the difference: money, facilities, leadership, expertise, needs, desires? Laying a strong foundation for a new program that will last beyond the current year requires creating and sustaining a team of lay people and staff to lead, advocate, suggest, strategize and problem-solve. All the time spent on planning and process may delay the initial inaugural program, but they will be beneficial in the long run. In any institution, staff come and go. It is the lay community that remains and that must embrace and lead new programs, institutional changes, and shifts in priorities and budgets. While a new program may rely heavily on one individual to spearhead it, it should not thereafter rely solely on any one individual—staff or lay leader. Building a team of advocates and lay leaders for family education will establish a strong foundation to build on for the future so that later, any additional professional that is hired (like the full-time principal here) will need to also embrace, understand and lead the program.

The second issue is the place of family education within the institution. Any new program will take time to become part of the infrastructure of a synagogue or other institution, but that process is critical to the continuing growth and support of the program. The following questions will help identify areas to be "fixed" to ensure a foundation for a vital program.

- Is there a Jewish family education committee?
- Is there at least one lay person who is identified with family education?
- Is family education a regular agenda item at the synagogue board meetings?
- If it is not a separate agenda item, where does it fall on the synagogue flowchart (e.g., as one of several subcommittees of the youth committee which is overseen by the education committee)?
- Is there a distinct family education budget? For staff? For programs?
- Is the professional family education staff full-time or part-time? Who supervises those educators?

The third issue is the need for professional development when family education is added, and the existing educational programming of a synagogue or school takes time. Family education is a skill and requires different training and personal attributes from working with children or adults alone. Teachers used to a school setting may or may not be able to deal with new types of programming. As with any change, understanding that people are initially reluctant or hesitant will facilitate a gradual and more successful addition of a new program and new philosophy.

The next issue involves appropriate reactions when a new program fails to thrive. Often, new programs begin without the above steps, processes and foundation-building beforehand. At any point in time, it is *not* too late to take a deep breath and start over, or take a few steps backwards to redevelop a team of advocates, bring all the key players into the process, and establish a place for family educators in the infrastructure. If it hasn't been done yet, do it!

Finally, we must plan for continuing maintenance and oversight. With the success, addition or growth of a new program, think about the role that a new program plays within the larger institution. As important as laying the groundwork for family education is, maintaining a keen political, big-picture eye on the institution is critical if our programs are to continue to receive support and thrive. The big picture includes making sure that as key lay people and professional people join the synagogue, they are nurtured as supporters of family education. As family education grows, watch that it does not do so to the detriment of another vital synagogue program. In the end, that hurts family education and the synagogue as a whole. As family education grows, continue to build and renew partnerships among the synagogue leadership, staff and laity. Launching family education is just step one. Step two is growing it and keeping it strong in the following year. Look at the entire synagogue as one *big* family, in which family education is just one of many children. The better the entire synagogue functions, the greater the chances are that each "child" will flourish.

Commentary by Jeff Schein

As an educational Rashi, I will start with my comments about the *peshat* (simple or literal meaning) of this case study. There are words and phrases in our text that puzzle, intrigue and confuse me. They demand interpretation. Here are some of the initial *kushiot* (problems) that emerge for me as I pore through this case study time and time again.

Road Block. Who or what is doing the blocking? Is it the funds? Perhaps there is a budget crunch in the synagogue we do not know about. Is it the family educator's energy? Perhaps he needs to do something during the summer to recharge his professional batteries. The vision of the new principal—is this vision different from or narrower than that of the rest of the community? Knowing which might help us to proceed.

The family part of the program. If the "family part" is a part, what is the whole? Does the author's concern for the "family part" of the program grow out of the concept that Jewish family education has a Jewish part, a family part and an education part? [1] Is that a helpful way to look at Jewish family education?

The rabbi and family educator show. The *peshat* here is that this is a bad thing—that something sinister is happening between the congregation and the professionals. The congregants don't believe that they are being dealt with honestly. There is a "snow job" going on here. Honest differences aren't being acknowledged. But there is a *sod* (hidden meaning) as well: I believe the rabbi and family educator secretly enjoy doing shows.

Davar a<u>h</u>er (one more matter) related to the "rabbi and family educator show." The author writes that they didn't succeed in "selling" Jewish family education. Why "selling" instead of other words—such as "educating", "convincing" or even "coercing"—that would also have worked in this *pasuk* (verse)?

Let me now offer some *midrash*, my own interpretation. I was once engaged in one of those frequent conversations in Jewish life about rabbis and congregations, when a smart social worker used a family systems metaphor to get at what she believed was the root of the problem. The rabbi was "enabling" the congregation to do less by choosing (even if unconsciously) to do more. I'm not suggesting that, with just a little *tzimtzum* (stepping back) on the part of the rabbi and family educator, hundreds of congregants will immediately step forward demanding to be empowered to do family education programs. But I do believe that there are some deeper dynamics of the "family system"

---

[1] Vicky Kelman, *Jewish Family Retreats: A Handbook*, The Melton Research Center of The Jewish Theological Seminary of America (New York) and The Shirley and Arthur Whizin Institute of the University of Judaism (Los Angeles), 1992, pp. 22-23

[2] Edwin Friedman, *Generation to Generation: Family Process in Church and Synagogue*, The Guilford Press (New York and London), 1986.

that we need to understand in regard to the congregation. The work of Edwin Fried-man, *alav ha-shalom* (may he rest in peace), can serve to illuminate these issues.[2]

We should also think about the relationship between the family educator and the principal. We must remember how new these relationships are in terms of our conventional professional staffing models. If the rabbi and educational director used to be the most significant professionals guiding Jewish education, things became more complex when a third party—the family educator—emerged. Now we have all the rich potentials and problems of a triangle. The development of such teams can lead to very different scenarios—the principal who has a very different understanding of family education and a strong sense of turf might drive the family educator from the synagogue, or the principal might become a competitor of the family educator. In either case, we are still at the beginning of our own learning curve of how to integrate the family educator into the professional team.

As much as our case study illustrates the cutting edge of what's new in Jewish education, it also touches on more timeless dilemmas of educational change. I don't remember a lot from my first graduate education class on curricular change, but I do remember two insights from the work of Lippit and Watson, *The Dynamics of Planned Change*. One is that significant educational changes take three to five years to accomplish.[3] The other is that the most difficult and unattended aspect of the change process is making sure that the change is systemic.[4] Family education can easily remain the pet project of one professional or particular population within the synagogue. Getting the whole community to sign off on the concept is a challenging, painstaking task. *Al regel ahat* (on one foot), it seems that in this case, people in this particular synagogue were so busy programming that they failed to attend to the wider culture-creating dimensions of their work, which inevitably must be addressed if the change is to affect the total congregation. (Edgar Schein's work is helpful in this regard.)

My colleague Daniel Pekarsky loves to quote John Dewey's saying that nothing is as practical as a good theory. In that vein, I'd like to raise a question about the wide canvas for family education that the rabbi speaks of—offering family education to the whole congregation, not just to the school, and targeting all populations in the synagogue. As Rashi, I might comment "*tafasta merubeh lo tafastah*"—if you reach for everything, you sometimes get nothing. From a congregant's perspective such breadth can be quite confusing and can even seem aimless and undisciplined. It sounds odd for me to say this, since I really am an advocate for a kind of intergenerational family education. But I recognize that this places a burden upon us of explaining and elucidating concepts and terms to others. To do so, we need a better-grounded theory than the rabbi's incantation of pedagogic and continuity jargon. For myself, I find the work of James White in *Intergenerational Religious Education* a helpful resource in this regard.

---

[3] Ronald Lippit, Jeanne Watson and Bruce Westley, *The Dynamics of Planned Change: A Comparative Study of Priciples and Techniques*, Harcourt, Brace (New York), 1958.

[4] Ibid., #3 & #4 emailed Jeff Schein 4/6/00

My final suggestion for bringing more *sh'lom bayit* (literally "peace at home") between the principal, family educator, congregation and educational staff is to teach them how to argue. A somewhat bothersome dynamic within this text is the hidden assumption that there is a single best way to do family education. Jewish family education is a very complex undertaking, with many different possibilities and understandings. I would like to see our burned-out family educator and bruised principal join together with involved and uninvolved parents in a year-long process of discovery and rejuvenation. Let them read selections from *First Fruit* by the Whizin Institute.[5] Let them go through the process of setting goals and determining priorities outlined in *Targilon: A Workbook for Charting a Course in Jewish Family Education.*[6] Shared vision and ownership may yet emerge from such a process, as well as a renewed commitment on the part of our family educator to the ideas that engaged him before the difficult dilemmas of Jewish living began to tarnish his dream.

[5] *First Fruit: A Whizin Anthology of Jewish Family Education*, Adrienne Bank and Ron Wolfson, eds., The Shirley and Arthur Whizin Institute for Jewish Family Life of the University of Judaism (Los Angeles), 1998.

[6] Leora W. Isaacs and Jeffrey Schein, *Targilon: A Workbook for Charting a Course in Jewish Family Education*, Mandell L. Berman Jewish Heritage Center for Research and Evaluation at Jewish Education Service of North America, Inc. (or JESNA; New York) and Jewish Reconstructionist Federation (Wyncote, PA), 1996.

Annotated Lesson Plan
(Notes for the Facilitator)

I. CASE OVERVIEW

- *Facilitator's Summary:* The new school director changes the family component of a well-established family education program, and the case writer (a congregant and quarter-time employee) feels that this typifies the problems with family education at their site. The case writer feels that she is always in a position of "selling" family education to the synagogue members and leaders. She struggles to root family education at her site and questions her own role.

- *Help the group determine what facts will be most useful in really understanding this case. It may be helpful to list them on the board.*

II. "WHAT IS THIS A CASE OF?"

In the groups with which we have studied this case, participants raised issues such as:

- Lack of communication
- Lack of common vision between professionals
- The challenge of personnel changes
- Insufficient buy-in from congregation, staff, lay people/Failure to build a strong enough base of support
- Burn out
- Lack of clarity re: definition of family education and individual roles
- A program too highly identified with one person
- Prioritizing the allocation of limited resources

Your group may come up with different or additional issues.

III. CASE ANALYSIS

- *At this point the discussion can go in any number of directions. You may want to begin by asking the group to choose one (or more) of the issues raised above as a focus by asking them which of the issues is most relevant to their practice. Or, as a facilitator, you may want to direct the conversation by choosing one (or more) of the issues raised and directing the discussion to meet your particular agenda for the group.*

- *For each of your discussion foci look at how that particular situation developed.*

  How do the players themselves (Dan, the rabbi, the writer) contribute to the situation?

  What do we know about family education at this site?

  What do we know about the educator? What is her attitude toward the program? What is her attitude toward the staff at her site?

- *What did the family educator do, with what results, risks and consequences?*

IV. INCORPORATING THE TEXT STUDY

- *How does our text study shed light on the case?* (See "Large Group Discussion Point" #1.)
- *Are there (other) Jewish value concepts that can help us see this issue from a Jewish perspective?* See the list of "Big Jewish Ideas" in the appendix. For example: *sh'lom bayit*–how does it apply to our situation?

V. CASE EVALUATION

- *In your experience, is this situation typical?*

  What is Family Education like at your site?

  Who are the opinion makers?

  Whom do you need on board?
- *What might be other ways of handling this situation? What are the risks and benefits of each?*
- *After our discussion would you refine your idea about what this is a case of?*
- *What lingering questions do you have?*

VII. CLOSURE—REFLECTION ON PRACTICE

Journaling and/or reflection in small groups is optional.

- *Choose a question that invites participants to connect the issues raised in the case discussion to their own practice of family education.*

  For example: Does family education have a strong base of support at your site? If so, how was this achieved? If not, how could it be improved?
- *Ask participants to extrapolate principles of practice–generalizations of good practice that could guide them in their own work.*
- *And/or have participants write about an issue from the case that was not discussed.*
- *And/or have participants reflect on the case study process: What new insights did you gain from our discussion? What part of the discussion did you find most challenging?*

CASE #5
JUDITH

Text: Who Is Wise?

TEXT: Pirkei Avot (Ethics of Our Fathers) 4:1 (Hebrew & English translation)

CONTEXT: We began this text study with a quick exercise. We asked participants to write down the name of the first person who came to mind when asked: "Of whom are you a student?" Then to write down the names of six more of their "teachers" (in the broadest sense of the word). We asked them to reflect on why those people came to mind. Then we went around and had each person say, "I am _____ (their name), student of _____ (the name of one of their teachers)."

QUESTIONS FOR STUDY IN HEVRUTA

1) How does this aphorism differ from a "typical" view of teaching?

2) What are the outer limits of this view of learning? (Who can be your teacher?)

3) What are the implications for us personally if we take this text seriously?

4) What are the implications for family education of viewing everyone as a potential teacher?

5) How can we acculturate people into this way of thinking about learning?

LARGE GROUP DISCUSSION POINT—for the facilitator:

In traditional Jewish text study we often find that the focus is on the unlearned. The message of the story of Rabbi Akiva's illiteracy until the age of forty, for example, is that it is never to late too learn. But what about the learned (in whatever field)? There are people of great learning among our "students" and it is important to recognize them and honor them. How can we do this when we are officially the "teacher"? How can we ask students to share with one another in a way that helps them see that they can learn from each other?

Text Study

From Whom Can We Learn?—Pirke Avot 4:1

Ben Zoma taught:

Who is wise? One who learns from every person,

As it is written,

'From all my teachers I have gained understanding.'" (Psalm 119:99)

-from Pirkei Avot 4:1

בֶּן זוֹמָא אוֹמֵר:

אֵיזֶהוּ חָכָם? הַלּוֹמֵד מִכָּל־אָדָם,

שֶׁנֶּאֱמַר—מִכָּל־מְלַמְּדַי הִשְׂכַּלְתִּי.

Case #5: Judith

The families ambled in to the second meeting of our monthly family education program for preschoolers and their parents. Some of the kids ran to the "warm-up" activity, which involved classifving and sorting different fruits and vegetables, while others held onto their parents' legs. The bagels were out, the adults were taking refuge in coffee, and the name tags were being decorated. In many ways, it was a typical Sunday morning for our group of twelve families. After everyone arrived we gathered for music, which for me is the easiest and most fun part of the morning. The children stare blankly. One three-year-old gets up to dance. A four-year-old begins clapping rhythmically. The adults are all singing enthusiastically. On this particular Sunday morning we are learning about *Sukkot*. The room reflects it—there is a *lulav* and an *etrog* on the table for families to touch and shake. The synagogue *sukkah* is adjacent to our room, shades the room and lets everyone know that somehow today is different. After singing we begin our activities for the day: making decorations for the *sukkah*, comparing lemons to *etrogs* and talking about people we would like to invite to be our *Sukkot* guests (in the spirit of *ushpizin*).

Although the children are all three- and four-year-olds, there is a wide developmental range among them. I try to provide open-ended projects, with varying degrees of complexity. One of the *sukkah* decoration activities involves tracing around children's and adults' bodies on large sheets of butcher paper. Some of the children draw complete faces on their people, with all the features, including ears and earrings, while others just scribble on a huge sheet of paper and then run off to another activity. (This diversity is fairly typical of preschoolers.)

It is now time for the children to remain with a teacher, and for me to have learning time with the adults. Most of the children separate quite easily; they have done it before. Sammy protests loudly, begins to cry and refuses to leave his parents. He then begins to have a full-fledged tantrum—kicking and throwing himself down on the floor. I suggest to his parents that one of them stay with Sammy in the children's group, with the hope that he will eventually develop a comfort level with the group and participate without his parents for this forty-five-minute time slot. His mom agrees to stay with him. He calms down.

As the adults take their places in their circle, refilling their coffee cups and becoming reacquainted, I get this familiar sinking feeling in the pit of my stomach, a leftover from our first session last month. How can I work with this very diverse group of nineteen adults in a deep, meaningful and non-threatening way?

Among the adults are three non-Jews and four Jews by choice; seven people are somewhat observant in their homes but are not very knowledgeable. One woman has recently become Orthodox. The group also includes a father who is a fairly mainstream Conservative Jew (some knowledge, some practice), and one mother who is a professional Jewish educator. Most are synagogue members, but there are a few who are unaffiliated, who found out about this program through word of mouth or an article in the community Jewish newspaper.

Judith, the professional Jewish educator, has lectured and published on a wide variety of Jewish topics. At the first session, when the adults were sharing their Jewish journeys, she proudly listed her accomplishments. In addition to reciting her list of publications and her impressive education, she also let it be known that she had chosen this program not for *her* benefit, but for her daughter's. She felt very comfortable with her level of Jewish knowledge and had no parenting issues to speak of. She felt, however, her daughter needed a Jewish program because she was enrolled in the university's preschool rather than in one of the community's Jewish schools.

After Judith spoke, the other parents seemed stunned. She was the next-to-last person to speak—fortunately, because otherwise I was sure that she would have silenced and intimidated the other participants.

After everyone left the first session, I realized that I also felt intimidated. Her Jewish background and knowledge were far superior to mine. What did I have to offer her? Would she be open when discussing parenting issues with other families? Would she feel that she had anything to learn? Could she contribute to the group in a positive way?

After the first session I decided to call Judith the next day. I told her that I wanted to let her know that she was a very valued member of the group and that I hoped that the group would be valuable for her as well. She replied that she didn't expect to learn anything Jewishly, but she very much wanted her daughter to participate, and she herself enjoyed the family projects. She told me in so many words that she would put up with the adult discussions.

Back to our second meeting: I gave a brief overview of the *Sukkot* holiday and had prepared handouts for the parents to read at home. We then discussed the custom of *ushpizin*—inviting our ancestors to reside with us in the *sukkah*. She was silent, though not disruptive, during the animated discussion.

As a Jewish family educator, I was nervous for two reasons. I did not want to screw up and make a mistake with such a witness in the room; basically, I didn't want to look incompetent. I also was nervous that she would be critical and that her forceful personality would affect the culture of the group.

In fact, she was neutral during the *Sukkot* discussion and a full participant during the family segment. But this session raised some important questions for me: What is the purpose of Jewish family education? Am I responsible for stimulating every parent, even the most Jewishly knowledgeable in the group? Is family education only for beginners, for families who don't know much Jewishly and whose parenting issues and skills are as diverse as their Jewish backgrounds?

At this point, my dilemma with this particular group is threefold:

1. How do I include this intimidating parent in a meaningful way?

2. How do I deal with such a diverse group—diverse in both Jewish parenting skills and Jewish knowledge—in a way that is inclusive and rich?

3. Is there a way to get a better handle on the wants and needs of this group?

Commentary by
Risa Munitz Gruberger

Let's take a close look at the case. It seems clear that our educator is qualified to design, organize and implement a program. She has covered all the bases. The families are welcomed with a diverse, non-threatening activity. Food is being served. Music is playing to create a friendly mood. The room reflects the content of the program. The program is designed to meet the developmental needs of the children. She handled Sammy and his temper tantrum quite well; her suggestion of having one parent stay with Sammy in the children's room was appropriate. Her quick thinking enabled her to move forward with the program.

Her challenges began as soon as the parents separated from their children and gathered to learn from our educator. For her, the group seemed to be less threatening when the family units were together. Some educators find it easier to "do" family education when the families are together, while others are more comfortable teaching parents and children separately. Teaching adults presents a different set of issues from teaching families or children. An expert in the field of adult learning, Betsy Katz, describes it best by saying that the field of adult Jewish education can be characterized by one word: "diversity." This simple fact points out the core issue—no two parents are alike, and an audience of adult learners will never be homogeneous. Therefore, an educator of adults can never be completely ready, and must make peace with the fact that he or she cannot fully prepare for a family teaching experience. This is hard for some educators to deal with. This takes courage.

Looking back to the case, the "sinking" feeling the educator experienced is normal. Even the most veteran educator can feel anxious before teaching. These moments of uncertainty show that the educator cares. Many teacher-student relationships are fraught with anxiety and fear. Both teacher and student feel an obligation to please. The teacher wants to please her students by imparting knowledge that is creative and accessible. The student wants to please the teacher by showing that he is engaged with the learning and that the learning has influenced him in a positive way. How rewarding it is for the teacher who is visited by a student who says, "You changed my life." When the fear is overcome, the relationship is quite powerful.

The student-teacher relationship provokes fear of the unknown. Our educator may have experienced that familiar feeling in the pit of her stomach because she was intimidated both by what she expected and by what she did not know. We can explore how she could have prepared better for the situation and the work she could have done prior to the event to ease her comfort level with the diversity of the group. We also

---

[10]Parker Palmer, *The Courage to Teach*, Jossey-Bass Publishers (San Francisco), 1998.

need to tackle the specific issue of the threat posed by the Jewish professional in her group.

Although we do not know why she felt so uneasy, some possible reasons are:

- she may be younger than most of the parents in the group;
- she may be fairly new to teaching adults or to family education;
- she may be afraid of what the adults will think of her;
- she may be afraid they will ask a question to which she will not know the answer; and
- she may be intimidated by and mistrustful of the Jewish professional in the group.

In addition, the "problem" parent's statement—that she is only there for her child and that she does not expect to learn anything—poses interesting challenges to the family educator. What is her obligation to that parent? Is it all right for a parent to attend the family programs only for the sake of her child? The core goal of every family education experience is encouraging new learning or adding onto a knowledge base. But is the family educator totally responsible for the participants' learning, and does she fail if learning does not take place? I would suggest not. It is commonly accepted in the field of education that learning is often a two-way relationship. If either the teacher or the student is not ready to both teach and learn, learning may not occur (although sometimes even the most skeptical parents or child may walk away from the experience knowing more or affected by it). Rabbi Harold Shulweis, Temple Valley Beth Shalom, often speaks about the impact on children of simply being on Jewish ground. He has no problem with children who attend services but spend the majority of their time in the synagogue lobby, because they are in a Jewish environment; better they should hang out in the synagogue lobby than the local mall. The same is true for participants in family education programs. No matter what a particular parent's intentions, at least she is there. Chances are greater for her to be touched Jewishly at synagogue than at the movies. And who knows, she may even learn something.

The truth is that learning in any setting is hard to measure, and we must rely on evaluation tools to discover whether our programs work. But certainly with respect to family education, the first step is to get people to our programs, where, we hope, the learning will occur. In this case, the Jewish professional assumes she will not learn anything, but stranger things have happened. All of us—even well-known Jewish professionals—have something to learn. Should the family educator devote her time to worrying about how to reach this particular parent? I think not. The reasons a particular parent chooses to attend a family program are not in our control, although knowing why she is there acts as a signal to her mindset. The more information we have about our families, the more successful we can be.

- There are some tools that would help the family educator to face similar situations. Parker Palmer, a nationally known educator, writes that there is an unspoken culture of fear in education.[1] In this case, Palmer would describe the educator's fear as a force that ultimately distanced her from working with the parents, the subject matter and herself. Acknowledging our fear leads to a more truthful atmosphere where real learning can take place.

- Although diversity in a family group can work for the educator, in this case it has worked against her. If she plans ahead, knowing that this is a group with many different backgrounds and interests, she will feel more prepared. She could ask herself the question, "How can I introduce the idea of *ushpizin* in a way that will be stimulating to all?" Often telling stories is a wonderful way to both introduce and reinforce concepts. While our veteran Jewish professional certainly knows all about *ushpizin*, she may not have heard every story relating to *ushpizin*. If the facilitator tells a personal story, she can open up a discussion in a non-threatening way by demonstrating that she has explored Judaism herself. If we share who we are, without fear, others may do the same.

- Acknowledging the diversity of the group can also serve to diminish the fears of both the educator and the group. She might say something like, "We are going to talk about one tradition of the holiday of *Sukkot*. Those of you that are familiar with *ushpizin*, please join me in teaching the group about a wonderful ritual. Those of you that have never heard of this tradition, please feel free to ask any questions. This is a really diverse group; we come from different backgrounds, and each of us has something to offer the others."

- I feel most challenged and rewarded when I accomplish my goals with a very diverse group. After all, a broader goal for the Jewish people at large is to be able to celebrate and learn together. The family group in this case is a microcosm of our entire Jewish community, consisting as it does of Jews from all denominations, Jews by choice, unaffiliated Jews and non-Jews who are married to Jews.

- The questions puzzling the educator—What is the purpose of family education? Is she responsible to stimulate all members of the group? Who is family education for?—all address a key facet of family education: modeling. I describe family education as assisting families to feel more comfortable and competent with Jewish knowledge and celebration. Through our program, we hope that all participating families, no matter where they start, will struggle, question and grow. This is a very human pursuit, and the family educator should model this pursuit. The fact she may not be able to answer all questions does not limit her as an educator; in fact, it strengthens her character. The parents in the group will see her courage as she seeks to grow her own Jewish knowledge. It is quite human for the leader of a group to say "I am not sure of the answer to your question. I will research it before we meet again. You research it, too, and we will see what we learned together." This empowers the parent as a learner and establishes a non-threatening forum for sharing new discoveries.

- Family education is for anyone who wants to learn. Just like students in a traditional classroom, participants in family education begin their learning from many different points, both as Jews and as families. It is the job of the family educator to move families along from the places where they begin. For example, take-home materials the educator prepares should mirror the diversity of the group. They should include both introductory material on *Sukkot* and materials for more advanced study of the holiday. This will help to speak to the whole group and yet meet individual needs. The educator could also ask the Jewish professional in the group whether she has any materials she would like to include in the packet.

- In this particular group, the mother who is considered "too Jewish" represents one type of parent that we work with. The courage required of family educators is the courage to work with all sorts of Jews, in all walks of life. We must accept the fact that some families are easier to work with than others. Family education is a discipline of human interaction and relationship-building. The way we interact with the families we work with should stem from our hearts.

- The educator in this case will be fortunate if she has an opportunity to have more experiences with this richly diverse group. She will benefit from such challenges by embracing their diversity, not trying to homogenize them.

Commentary by Cindy Dolgin

The author of our case study describes a feeling that is common to both novices and veterans in the field of Jewish family education—anxiety over facilitating meaningful adult discussions.

Despite my own years of teaching experience and ongoing learning, I still question my ability to command enough pearls from the vast pool of Jewish knowledge, not to mention my skills as a teacher of adults and ability to remain neutral and non-judgmental as a discussion facilitator. I break into a cold-hot-cold sweat when the informal dialogue steers off subject or beyond my mastery. What if a group member asks a question or raises a subject leading right into one of my many gaping knowledge-holes? What if I can't provide an answer to a simple question? And worst of all, what if a "student" knows an answer that I, the "teacher," do not? How will that affect my legitimacy in the eyes of the participants?

That ever-nagging fear of being upstaged or outsmarted by an adult participant began to abate with time. Through on-the-job experience, I came to expect and even to anticipate that there would almost always be at least one participant in the group with more knowledge than I in some critical aspect of the discussion. Perhaps a parent participant would be a public school teacher with a keen understanding of human development, or a psychologist who could dance circles around my ability to draw out the real issues and who would be skilled at bringing closure to a discussion right on time. Maybe there would be an Israeli who would notice my lack of confidence when reciting *brachot* aloud, or a parent who had chosen to forgo a career to dedicate full time and effort toward raising her children while I wondered how my kids were faring in my absence.

What if a professional Jew came to the group for the sake of her child, although she has already incorporated Jewish ritual observance into everyday life and has no child-rearing issues to speak of? Maimonides, the great Jewish philosopher, wrote, "Disciples increase the teacher's wisdom and broaden his mind. The sages said, 'Much wisdom have I learned from my teachers, more from my colleagues, but from my pupils have I learned most of all.'"[1] This ancient Jewish wisdom helped me to accept and eventually to embrace the fact that, as a family educator, my role is not to provide all the right answers, but to create the forum for participants to grow—sometimes by learning, sometimes by teaching, sometimes by giving, sometimes by getting, sometimes as individuals and other times as a family. By putting my own fears and insecurities aside, I could seek out opportunities to capitalize on the wisdom and experience that each parent brings to the group. After several years of investing countless hours trying to nail down every fact, ritual, historical link, and bit of information that might come

---

[1] Francine Lagsbrun, *Voices of Wisdom: Jewish Ideals and Ethics for Everyday Living*, Jonathan David Publishers, Inc. (Middle Village, NY), 1980, p. 263.

up during a family education session, I refocused my energies on creating a safe and respectful environment where everyone had an opportunity to grow in some way.

Simple as it may sound, it was a breakthrough moment for me when I deeply understood that, in any given family education setting, every family brings with it a unique story and its own specific goals. We are all at different points on the spectrum, we each have different areas of expertise and personal experience and we all can grow, but different people are prepared to and interested in growing in different ways. Some want to *know* more, while others want to *do* more. Some want to improve the quality of family time, while some may seek a quality Jewish peer experience for their children or themselves. All have different—and good—reasons for participating in a Jewish family education program..

As John Gardner notes in his classic work, *Excellence: Can We Be Equal and Excellent Too?*, "The good society is not one that ignores individual differences but one that deals with them wisely and humanely." [2] The role of the family educator in this particular case study is to find the way to moderate the monthly gatherings so that everyone—whether non-Jew, Jew-by-choice, or Jew-by-vocation—feels safe, valued and able to participate comfortably when ready.

The parent who is an accomplished Jewish professional and who has no parenting issues to speak of need not be a threat to the balance of the group or to the authority of the family educator. During the adults-only study sessions, the leader serves as the critical link: She allocates air time, decides whom to call on, and tries to ensure that all members of the group receive ample opportunities to speak. David A. Garvin, professor of business administration at the Harvard Business School and co-editor of *Education for Judgement: The Artistry of Discussion Leadership*, offers some good advice to family educators about the ethical dilemmas of the discussion process. "Protection of the discussion process comes first, because it is the bedrock of effective teaching. Without faith that the rules are secure and their personal safety nets will not be withdrawn, students are unlikely to continue to invest themselves in the discussion either actively or enthusiastically." [3]

While participants with a great deal of expertise often tend to dominate the discussion, the "expert" parent in this particular case did not. On the contrary, she was quiet, leaving the family educator disappointed that this mother was barely willing to "put up with the adult discussions." I see more than one way to interpret the parent's silence. Considering her own professional background, she may not be accustomed to being on the learning end of the classroom, and she may just need time to adjust. Or it may be something else. It is up to the family educator to do all in her power to help this and *all* participants feel comfortable and valued.

---

[2] John W. Gardner, *Excellence: Can We Be Equal and Excellent Too?*, New York: Perennial Library, Harper and Row, 1961, p. 88.

[3] C. Roland Christensen, David A. Garvin and Ann Seet, eds., *Education for Judgement: The Artistry of Discussion Leadership*, Boston: Harvard Business School, 1991, pp. 287-302.

Realistic and flexible expectations lead to longevity and contentment in the field of family education. A family educator who expects to please all the adult participants every moment of the program is ignoring the fact that people have a variety of reasons for joining this monthly group and a variety of learning styles. How interesting that the leader does not feel like a failure because some children draw faces and earrings while others scribble or because some children separate easily while one child throws a tantrum. On the contrary, she recognized that such diversity is fairly typical of pre-schoolers. Her failure to realize that there is a similar diversity among adults leads to her feelings of disappointment.

A realistic family educator would be grateful, though surprised, if all participants in the group were equally interested in all three components of this particular family education program: parent-child learning, adult learning and preschool learning. She would be content if she knew that everyone came out of interest in *two* of the components. If one or two families chose to participate in this program in order for the child to have a positive Jewish peer experience *and* for the parent and child to share a positive Jewish experience, she should be a happy family educator. Her cup is, as they say, more than half full.

That is not to say I would simply ignore the professional Jewish parent. David A. Garvin recommends that the leader be mindful to offer the "expert student" airtime equal to the other participants', tapping into that resource at the right times to enrich the experience of others.[4] For example, the leader might offer an opportunity for each group member to share an impression, recollection or experience of celebrating *Sukkot* from their childhood or adult lives. Such an invitation would offer the more Jewishly knowledgeable participants (including, but not exclusively, this particular parent) an informal "teaching" moment as they describe their family's authentic Jewish celebrations at home, while not putting others, who have never celebrated *Sukkot*, on the spot. To deal effectively with the Jewish diversity in the group, the leader might also say, "Before I get started, and to insure I cover the details that might interest you, what questions do you have about *Sukkot* or the other Jewish fall holidays? We'll write your questions on the board, with an eye toward covering the details that you're interested in."

Although the family educator has already told this particular parent that she is a valued member of the group, it is up to the family educator to make her *feel* it. The leader might explicitly ask what kind of role this mother can foresee taking. For example, she might be interested in periodically taking on a more formal leadership role, either by teaching or by moderating a discussion. Although this parent doesn't expect to *learn* anything Jewishly, she might add to the learning of others, not only about Jewish facts, but about her own personal Jewish journey. And then, you never know if this professional Jew and her family will form new friendships in the group, if common parenting issues may arise, or if new insights from the vast pool of Jewish knowledge may pop up. As long as the family educator holds the door wide open, this parent and all others will feel comfortable determining their own levels of participation.

The writer asks, "Is there a way to get a better handle on the wants and needs of this group?" Having participants fill out a simple but thorough intake survey prior to the start of the course is an excellent way to learn something of the backgrounds and expectations of participant families. Although this may sound intimidating, the *Bagels, Blocks and Beyond* parent education program in Suffolk County, Long Island, has been asking participating parents to fill out a fifteen-minute intake survey prior to the start of its two-year monthly family education program, and no parent has ever balked. At the course's conclusion, participants always enjoy seeing their old responses and gauging how far they've come after two years of learning and experimentation, incorporating new knowledge and skills into the family's repertoire.[5] Alternatively, the family educator might offer a ten-minute opportunity for the participants to write a response to the question, "In what ways do you hope this program will have an impact on you, your child and the life of your family?" The educator can then use the narrative responses to set the agenda for the sessions and to set her own expectations at reasonable levels.

Embracing and understanding the needs of each individual and family invariably reaps rewards for participants who sometimes give and sometimes get, each at his or her own pace. It also leads to those welcomed "*nachas* (pleasure) moments" for the family educator who can see the unique impact that her program makes on individual children, adults and families and on the group as a whole. Realistic and flexible expectations increase both the results and the rewards.

---

[1] For more information about the Bagels, Blocks, and Beyond intake survey, contact SAJES, the Suffolk Association of Jewish Educational Services at 777 Larkfield Road, Commack, NY 11725; phone (516) 549-2626.

Annotated Lesson Plan
(Notes for the Facilitator)

I. **CASE OVERVIEW**

- *Facilitator's Summary:* A monthly family education program for preschoolers and their parents involves a diverse group of families. The range of knowledge among the adults is a challenge to this case writer. One parent in particular intimidates the narrator because of her vast Jewish knowledge.

- *Help the group determine what facts will be most useful in really understanding this case. It may be helpful to list them on the board.*

II. **"WHAT IS THIS A CASE OF?"**

In the groups with which we have studied this case, participants raised issues such as:

- Diversity within a group of families of Jewish knowledge, of parenting styles, of commitment, of children's abilities (age-related)
- Conflicting expectations
- Dealing with a challenging participant
- Trying to please everyone
- Defining family education—Is it just for beginners?
- Managing group dynamics
- Judging success
- Assessing the needs of a group
- The vulnerability of the professional

Your group may come up with different or additional issues.

III. **CASE ANALYSIS**

- *At this point the discussion can go in any number of directions. You may want to begin by asking the group to choose one (or more) of the issues raised above as a focus by asking them which of the issues is most relevant to their practice. Or, as a facilitator, you may want to direct the conversation by choosing one (or more) of the issues raised and directing the discussion to meet your particular agenda for the group.*

- *For each of your discussion foci look at how that particular situation developed.*

  How do the players themselves (Judith and the writer) contribute to the situation?

  What do we know about the educator?

  What is her attitude toward the program?

  What is her attitude toward the participants (adults and children) and to

Judith in particular?

- *What did the family educator do, with what results, risks and consequences?*

- *How do you think the situation appeared to other participants and why do you think so?*

IV. INCORPORATING THE TEXT STUDY

- *How does our text study shed light on the case?* (See "Large Group Discussion Point" #1)

- *Are there (other) Jewish value concepts that can help us see this issue from a Jewish perspective?* See the list of "Big Jewish Ideas" in the appendix. For example: *anivoot, kavod, klal yisrael, talmud torah, tochecha—how do they apply to our situation?*

V. CASE EVALUATION

- *In your experience, is this situation typical?*

- *What might be other ways of handling this situation? What are the risks and benefits of each?*

- *After our discussion would you refine your idea about what this is a case of?*

- *What lingering questions do you have?*

VI. CLOSURE—REFLECTION ON PRACTICE

Journaling and/or reflection in small groups is optional.

- *Choose a question that invites participants to connect the issues raised in the case discussion to their own practice of family education.*

  For example: What are your vulnerabilities? How do you play to your strengths? What do you need to strengthen, and how would you go about it?

- *Ask participants to extrapolate principles of practice–generalizations of good practice that could guide them in their own work.*

- *And/or have participants write about an issue from the case that was not discussed.*

- *And/or have participants reflect on the case study process: what new insights did you gain from our discussion? What part of the discussion did you find most challenging?*

CASE # 6
ALAN

Text: Rav Shimi & Rav Papa

TEXT: Babylonian Talmud, Tractate Taanit 9b (Aramaic & English translation)

CONTEXT:
- In the time when this anecdote took place the relationship between a teacher and student (in this setting) was a very intense one. The student learned with his teacher all day, every day, for most of his life.
- Rav Papa was Rav Shimi's teacher.
- To *makshe* can mean both to ask a lot of questions and to dispute.
- When it says that Shimi found Papa "fallen on his face" it refers to the recitation of the confessional prayer known as *tahanun*. In Talmudic times this prayer was a completely private, thoroughly intimate, spontaneous moment of supplication where one lay prostrate on the ground. To be overheard at this moment was akin to overhearing someone in therapy or confession today.

QUESTIONS FOR STUDY IN HEVRUTA

1) What happens in this story? Paraphrase it in writing.
2) What is this story about? How would you title it?
3) Why might a student ask a lot of questions? What could a teacher think of such a student?
4) What does this text imply about learning?

LARGE GROUP DISCUSSION POINTS—for the facilitator

1) The silence of Shimi. Shimi's vow might imply that either he never asked another question of Papa or that he never spoke again. In either case, the silence of Shimi is deafening, and the textual ambiguity is purposeful—we don't know what Papa meant or what Shimi understood. What we do know is that there is poor communication between teacher and student. Shimi is guessing at his teacher's meaning (as are we, the readers). Papa doesn't speak with Shimi; rather ,he beseeches God. The irony is that he thinks God has answered his prayers when we readers know that actually Shimi has simply overheard him. Shimi's actions may look like a kind of *teshuva,* and Papa may have felt that his prayers were answered, but the whole thing is a big "miss" because no one is clear about what happened, and they don't ever speak with one another about the problem.

2) Communication. Let us extend the discussion of poor communication between teacher and student to include the group dynamics in family education programs. Students often come at teachers with lots of questions and may even seem to be hostile in their questioning. We, the educators, might feel embarrassed about our own lack of knowledge. We might resent being challenged in front of others. We might feel attacked, overwhelmed or even unable to get through enough material because of students' questions. How do we communicate with them and find an appropriate way to express our feelings about their behavior?

Text Study

Babylonian Talmud, Tractate Taanit 9b

Rav Shimi Bar Ashi was studying with Rav Papa [his teacher][1]
And was "*makshe*"[2] him a great deal,
One day he [Shimi] found him [Papa] on his face[3] and heard him say:
"Compassionate one save me from the embarrassment of Shimi."
He [Shimi] took it upon himself [in a vow] to be silent
And never "*makshe*"d him [Papa] again.

רַב שִׁימִי בַּר אַשִׁי הֲוָה
שְׁכִיחַ קַמֵּיה דְּרַב פָּפָא
הֲוָה מַקְשֵׁי לֵיה טוּבָא.
יוֹמָא חַד חַזְיֵיה דִּנְפַל
עַל אַפֵּיה: שַׁמְעֵיה דְּאָמַר
רַחֲמָנָא לִיצְלָן מִכִּיסוּפָא דְּשִׁימִי.
קַבֵּיל עֲלֵיה שְׁתִיקוּתָא,
וְתוּ לֹא אַקְשֵׁי לֵיה.

---

[1] This type of relationship was a very intense one, where the student learned with his teacher all day, every day, for the rest of his life.

[2] *Maksh* means both "to ask questions" and "to dispute".

[3] "Falling on one's face" refers to the confessional prayer called "***tahanun***." In Talmudic times this prayer was a completely private, thoroughly intimate, spontaneous moment of supplication where one lay prostrate on the ground. To be overheard at this point was akin to overhearing someone in therapy or confession today.

Case #6—Alan

"With an attitude like that you probably have very few friends," Alan muttered, under his breath but loud enough for the entire group to hear. I had just commented on what I felt was the mixed message of a Christmas tree in a Jewish home. I was stunned and embarrassed.

We were in the middle of the adult discussion portion of our once-a-month *shabbat* morning family education program. That year, twelve families—one or both parents and their preschool children—came together for a two-and-a-half-hour program at the synagogue. Half of the parents were intermarried, while the others were both Jewish. About three quarters were synagogue members; the others were not yet affiliated. Each meeting consisted of parent/child time, a separate adult study time and a short *shabbat* service.

I had been facilitating this holiday-based program for three years. Although I had had more than fifteen years of classroom teaching, this was my first foray into teaching adults. While I was more than willing to admit that I did not have the answer to everything, I always felt on shaky ground in the adult session. Alan's comment fed right into these feelings.

Here we were, sitting in a circle in the library of a mid-size Conservative synagogue. As the facilitator of the program, I brought in materials each month to stimulate discussion on a variety of levels. The program had two goals. The first was to provide an opportunity for parents and their preschoolers to have fun Jewishly together, then continue to share the materials at home after a session. The second goal was to present holiday mate.ial on an adult level in a non-threatening setting. I wanted to encourage discussion of family issues related to the holidays and of how to involve preschoolers in the preparing for and celebrating of Jewish holidays.

The twelve families had been meeting monthly for the past four months. The discussion this month focused on *Chanukah*, although Alan's outburst came at the moment we were talking about Christmas celebrations in Jewish homes. Alan, a Jew by birth, and his wife Caron, a Jew by choice, showed up each month with their three-year-old daughter, Dana. Caron always participated more eagerly than her husband in the parent discussions, describing how important it was to infuse their home with Judaism and make it a place of joy and celebration for their daughter. Alan, on the other hand, had sat through the previous sessions with his arms crossed over his chest, emanating waves of hostility. It seemed as if he was always waiting for proof that any Jewish issues were relevant or important to him. He frequently disapproved of my comments or disagreed with someone else in the group. His comments ranged from "I can't believe you would say that" or "That would never work in our house" to "Maybe you just haven't experienced this." He seemed to have an opinion about everything. Strangely enough, no one in the group ever commented on or challenged his remarks. Even his wife made no attempt to temper his hostility. I was not sure if I should confront him, or if doing so would open up the floor for the soapbox preaching he seemed to desire.

However, this personal attack on me, which seemed to come from left field, seemed too egregious to ignore. Still reeling, I told him I did not understand the relevance of his comment to our discussion. "It's clear," he stated, "that you don't have your finger on the pulse of the intermarried family. It seems you are insensitive to the pull of a Christmas tree even if the non-Jewish partner has converted to Judaism. The problem with many Jews is that they can see things only through Jewish eyes and are insensitive to what someone has left behind!"

After Alan's outburst I was so disoriented that I just wanted to deflect the discussion from me and from the issue. Luckily, it was almost time to join the children and other staff for the *shabbat* service. I asked if anyone had any other comments. No one commented on Alan's outburst. The discussion was picked up by a non-Jewish participant who wanted to discuss the merits of a Christmas tree. Somehow we stumbled to the end of the discussion and finished the session.

I later described some of the problems I had with Alan to the rabbi, who rolled his eyes as if to say that he also had dealt with him. It was beginning to appear to me that I was dealing with a challenging participant rather than a personal attacker. Nevertheless, my skills as a facilitator had been undermined by Alan, who—amazingly enough—signed up for another year.

Commentary by Rachel E. Sisk

This case raises several deeper issues than that of a Christmas tree in a Jewish home. We know these issues are significant, because the behaviors displayed within the group in the Christmas tree discussion occur on an ongoing basis. These deeper issues are:

- Interfaith sensitivities and common language

- Personal feelings about Judaism

- Group facilitation and self-confidence

Interfaith sensitivities and common language. Although the Christmas tree issue is not the primary one in this case, it is symbolic of the environment in which family education takes place today. We live in a world where we cannot assume that the families in our Jewish family education programs are Jewishly knowledgeable or even that they are Jewish. The family educator in this case was fortunate to know in advance that half of the families attending the program described in the case are intermarried. More often than not we do not have such information and must figure it out for ourselves. Therefore, more than ever before, we must be careful and cautious in the way we use language and the things we say.

The family educator in this case chose to discuss with her group the "mixed message" of Christmas celebrations, and Christmas trees in particular, in a Jewish home. We do not know, however, what that discussion actually entailed. Colleagues who work with interfaith families teach us to define terminology, or at least to articulate assumptions before beginning a conversation like this one, which has the potential of becoming quite emotional. For example, celebrating Christmas can mean decorating the home with a tree, ornaments, tinsel and holly to one family, exchanging gifts to another, and a spiritual experience to a third. These kinds of celebrations may have vastly different significance and meaning to the people describing them as well as the people listening.

A group leader needs to make sure everyone starts on as close to the same page as possible, in groups of Jews as well as in interfaith groups. Facilitators can do this at the outset through defining the language to be used. In this example, without defining "celebrating Christmas"—or even what is meant by "Christmas tree"—it is difficult for everyone involved in the conversation to share the same vision. The same holds true for Hebrew phrases and Jewish calendar or life cycle events.

As "trained Jews," family educators are in the business of imparting Jewish knowledge and promoting Jewish lifestyles. We do not always see things the way the rest of the world does, particularly around interfaith issues. Therefore, it behooves us to step into the shoes of our constituents for at least a few moments before we push forward with our own agendas. If we can understand where they are coming from, even if we disagree, it will help us show greater respect for them in the conversations that follow. In turn, they are more likely to show us greater respect and listen less defensively.

Personal feelings about Judaism. Although Alan's words may come across as hostile in both this and previous incidents, they might be a mask for his discomforts. At the point we meet him, he appears to be dealing with several issues that have been unrecognized by the group's facilitator. From his comments, Alan seems to feel ambivalent about being Jewish and needs support, validation and clarification, even if he cannot express those needs. On the one hand, he feels that he is being a supportive and flexible husband, particularly in regard to having a Christmas tree in his home. His comments, however, also show hesitancy about this decision. He appears conflicted about Judaism in his home, and specifically about his wife's commitment to creating a Jewish home. Aside from the Christmas tree issue, her dedication to Judaism may be stronger than his own, which may be quite threatening to him.

The question Alan struggles with may very well be "Where and how does Judaism fit comfortably into my life?" As family educators our challenge, at its very base, is to help people deal with the question—the place and role of Judaism in one's family life. First, however, we have to recognize that the question is being asked. Most of the time, as with Alan, the question is unspoken. Sometimes we have to look beyond the surface to determine the larger issues, despite the difficulties involved.

We must also rise to the challenge of bringing what may have begun as a personal exploration into the expanded realm of the family. In this case, because a marriage is indeed a joint journey that the partners agree to take, Alan and his wife must answer the question "Where and how does Judaism fit comfortably into *our* lives?" We can help couples recognize and respond to the question on a basic level, but we may not be able to do so alone. We cannot have all the answers and all the expertise all the time. As family educators we must know when referrals are necessary to complement our work and must not be afraid to use them. A rabbi, a counselor or even a book may be able to help families find their way to a comfortable Judaism beyond our interactions with them.

Group facilitation and self-confidence. Working with groups is tough, and groups of adults are very different from groups of children. Adults have strong opinions that they are not afraid to voice. Adults can tell you that you are wrong and why. Adults can be intimidating because of their knowledge. But without adults there can be no family education. So, how do we let them share their thoughts while feeling comfortable in our role as facilitator and confident in our ability to impart knowledge? We set ground rules, clarify roles and build relationships.

From the case we understand that Alan is outspoken and antagonistic. We are told that the facilitator questions her abilities with adults, and that Alan's wife, like the rest of the group, is passive when it comes to dealing with Alan's frequent outbursts. This is not an uncommon situation, although it is often uncomfortable. Alan's disruptive behavior could be guided, however, by ground rules that everyone in the group implements. The creation of a safe space where people do not feel attacked and everyone is allowed to share is critical to the success of any group. The facilitator, as the one in charge, has the responsibility for ensuring that this takes place both at the outset and throughout the group sessions.

Alan needs to find an appropriate way to speak in the group without marginalizing others (including the facilitator) or monopolizing the discussion. If the facilitator develops a relationship with him independent of the group, she can ask him to take on a leadership role within the group. He is more likely to take her seriously when she shows him individual attention. He needs to know that he is heard and that his thoughts matter. Building trust is the key to every relationship, and it begins with active listening and positive reinforcement.

Similarly, if the facilitator develops an individual relationship with his wife, she might provide insights into Alan's behavior that would help the facilitator deal better with Alan within the group. Through such a relationship the facilitator might also show Alan that he was not being singled out, show his wife that her unique role was recognized and gain valuable information about how she could facilitate the group with greater self-confidence. She could also see the larger picture more clearly, perhaps giving her the ability to refer the couple out to another professional.

The rabbi of the synagogue is an important source for the facilitator—not only as a resource and referral, but as a member of her professional team. A relationship with a trusted colleague is critical to our work as family educators. Having someone to go to— with whom to share feelings, brainstorm, role play, gather ideas and be heard—helps us to be in touch with ourselves and the community in which we work. It keeps us on our toes and energized by ensuring that we do not operate in a vacuum. When the facilitator in this case went to the rabbi and shared her experience with Alan, he communicated to her that he had had similar encounters and clearly understood the incident. He may have been unavailable at that particular moment to engage in extended conversation, but she can approach him at another time for feedback, insight and the closure she needs to continue.

When most of us are mastering a new skill area, self-confidence comes slowly as we gain experience, knowledge and practice. As family educators we have many techniques to acquire and, as we see in this case, multiple hats to wear: group worker, interpreter, referral source, teacher, friend, confidant and role model. There will always be surprises and challenges, whether in the form of people, institutions or situations. Our task is to handle them with as much patience, confidence and insight as possible, arming ourselves with information and relationships that can help us along the way.

Commentary by Ron Muroff

The Rabbis of the Talmud distinguished among four different levels of interpretation:

- *Peshat* = literal meaning
- *Remez* = "hint," veiled allusions
- *Drash* = homiletical interpretation
- *Sod* = hidden, the mystical interpretation

These four interpretive methods are known by the acronym *PaRDeS*, which means orchard. If one understands the Torah as a "tree of life," these four levels of interpretation represent the orchard of Torah.

In that same spirit, I would like to offer four kinds of commentary in response to our case. Indeed, we can use the paradigm taught by the rabbis in evaluating family education. Life, like a Torah text, is multi-layered, with different meanings gleaned from literal, hinted, hidden and homiletic possibilities.

For this particular case the "orchard" of commentary centers on four elements of family education: preparation, reflections, dynamics and supervision. The mnemonic remains *PaRDeS*. In "Preparation" I reflect on the training and orientation of the family educator. "Dynamics" examines the relationships between the family educator and the group and among group members. "Supervision" considers the role of the supervisor in particular and the sponsoring institution in general in the success of family education. "Reflections" explores insights gained from the practice of family education and how those insights can enlarge the capacities of the family educator.

Preparation. Several aspects of the case touch on the nature of training family educators. Here the family educator is an experienced Hebrew school teacher but is relatively inexperienced in and uncomfortable with teaching adults. Quite possibly this professional received little or no instruction as she made a transition to a new position. Often, in loosely organized systems such as synagogues, people are placed into positions based on urgent need and past accomplishments without sufficient attention to the challenges and subtleties they are likely to face.

Teaching adults is profoundly different from teaching children, and teaching adults and children together is different from both. Training is required to teach in all three settings. In particular, the skills of family educators need to be developed or enhanced in areas such as classroom management, goal setting, the use of time and the art of facilitation.

An educator who is accustomed to teaching preschoolers can often interpret the actions of an opinionated adult participant like Alan as a personal attack. Even the most difficult preschooler is not as threatening to the authority of a teacher as a challenging parent in a family education setting. Learning to manage such participants necessitates a full repertoire of management skills. Invariably, there is an Alan in every group. (See "Dynamics" below.)

While flexibility is a requirement in family education, identifying specific goals is important, too, as it is in every educational setting. Goals should be framed from the perspective of the participants. What skills, ideas and experiences do we want adults and children to explore and master? If goals are too general and materials or activities do not further the attainment of discrete goals, the family educator may find herself being led by the group. Activities and discussions alone do not constitute family education. In the hands of a master, family education is a shared—though guided—journey.

The art of facilitation is a critical skill for family educators. There is a profound distinction between a skilled facilitator and a capable moderator: Whereas a moderator's role is to establish and maintain rules of engagement, a facilitator has a plan. Sharing the Torah, setting the parameters, offering guidance, then withdrawing to allow the group to interact is what makes family education work. In many ways, successful family education depends on the facilitator's knowing when to engage a topic or person and when not to.

Dynamics. Much of the work of family education takes place in the interactions between the family educator and the participants and interactions among the participants.

One strategy used in some settings to establish the relationship between the facilitator and the participants is a pre-program interview, an opportunity to outline the program, explore the background and expectations of the participants and determine whether the participants and the program are a good match.

With or without a pre-program interview, it is important to institute guidelines for the roles of facilitator and participant, such as confidentiality and mutual respect, which should be firmly enforced. Enforcement is largely the responsibility of the facilitator. A group can rarely manage itself, particularly with respect to a person as strong and opinionated as Alan, and a participant who criticizes one of his outbursts would risk becoming the focus of a subsequent outburst.

A group of parents like the one described in our case is complex—composed of different sub-groups and individuals, each with his own background and expectations. (For more on the importance of biography in education, see Diane Shuster's work on personal stories in *First Fruit*, edited by Adrienne Bank and Ron Wolfson.[1]) The dynamics of a typical family education group include those between men and women, Jews and non-Jews and affiliated and not yet affiliated.

My own experience teaching separate and mixed-gender groups confirms what some popular studies have indicated regarding the differences between how men and women learn. Men tend to be more argumentative, women more collaborative; men more interested in issues of fact and theory, women more comfortable in the realms

[1] *First Fruit: A Whizin Anthology of Jewish Family Education*, Adrienne Bank and Ron Wolfson, eds., The Shirley and Arthur Whizin Institute for Jewish Family Life (Los Angeles), 1998, Chapter 4.

of the spiritual and practical. Perhaps the differences between Alan and his wife Caron that the family educator noted had to do with their genders as much as their differing Jewish backgrounds. In this regard, it does not surprise me that Alan chose to sign up for another year. Why not? Perhaps challenging the (female) "expert" was what he enjoyed most.

In a mixed group of Jews and non-Jews, participants often show a great deal of deference to the Jewish members, perhaps due to a shared assumption (often erroneous) that the Jews know more. This can cause discomfort for non-Jews who may be bashful about asking basic questions and for Jewish participants who have ambivalent feelings about Jewish identity. In particular, those Jews who are "not-affiliated-yet" (a very Rosenzweigian phrase!) may have a personal history with the organized Jewish community that is very different from that of participants who are confident and at home in the synagogue.

On occasion, however, Jewish participants in family education programs defer to non-Jewish participants in an effort not to offend them and not to sound judgmental.

Supervision. It is interesting that, in our case, the family educator did not confer with the rabbi until after the incident with Alan. I know how busy rabbis are but still question why the facilitator did not meet regularly with the rabbi. Indeed, there is no mention of any supervision. Even if the rabbi is not the facilitator's supervisor, meetings with him could be helpful for both professionals.

Regular supervisory sessions could be a means to explore issues such as the following:

- the fact that, after three years of teaching adults, the facilitator still feels "on shaky ground";
- the educator's uncertainty regarding confronting Alan;
- handling conflict in general;
- lesson planning;
- the role of the facilitator; and
- group dynamics.

Supervision could be a useful opportunity for the facilitator to explore areas of concern and to receive positive feedback and support. Of course, effective supervision entails more feedback than "rolled eyes."

When an institution like a synagogue becomes involved in family education, but does not develop the structures—like supervision—to sustain the work, the initiative is destined to fall short of its potential. Without ongoing supervision and other contacts with professionals in the institution or agency, the family educator is on her own, unable to benefit from the perspectives of others who are serving the same community.

Reflections. The keen self-awareness of the family educator in this case is striking, especially her candor about her feelings of incompetence and insecurity. An encouraging sign of her growth is her thought, expressed at the end, that she was "dealing with a challenging participant rather than a personal attacker."

While the facilitator might explore some of her insights in supervision (as discussed above), family educators need other forums in which to share such perceptions. Developing a community of peers and mentors is critical. Conferences such as the Whizin Institute and CAJE[2] promote the exploration of experiences and the study of common themes in family education. Some communities have developed circles of family educators who meet regularly to reflect and collaborate. Promoting the use of case studies like this one is still another way for practitioners to examine the art of family education and consider their own practice.

Peer groups can serve as useful and safe arenas in which to re-examine deeply held beliefs and assess their impact on family education. However painful it was for the family educator to hear Alan's final comment, it is certainly appropriate to consider his view that "the problem with many Jews is that they can see things only through Jewish eyes and are insensitive to what someone has left behind!" One can only imagine what kind of creative curriculum a group of family educators could develop in response to the very real challenge of seeing the world through different sets of lenses.

Family educators need not walk their journeys alone. Family education is a profoundly collaborative enterprise. Reflections in the company of colleagues lead to renewal, individual and communal.

---

[2]The Shirley and Arthur Whizin Institute for Jewish Family Life of the University of Judaism (Los Angeles) and Conference on Alternatives in Jewish Education (or CAJE).

Annotated Lesson Plan
(Notes for the Facilitator)

I. CASE OVERVIEW

- *Facilitator's Summary:* A mid-size Conservative synagogue hosts a monthly, holiday-based, Shabbat morning family education program for twelve preschoolers and their parents. Though she has been facilitating this particular program for three years, the case writer experiences the "adults only" portion of the program as challenging. In this case, one parent, Alan, challenges the case writer with a personal attack.

- *Help the group determine what facts will be most useful in really understanding this case. It may be helpful to list them on the board.*

II. "WHAT IS THIS A CASE OF?"

In the groups with which we have studied this case, participants raised issues such as:

- Dealing with interfaith families in a Jewish educational setting
- A challenging participant
- Addressing the personal "baggage" of participants
- Group facilitation, group dynamics
- Teachers of children becoming teachers of adults
- Confidence and vulnerability of the professional
- Unique challenges of ongoing groups
- Diversity among participants
- Surprise (being caught off guard)

Your group may come up with different or additional issues.

III. CASE ANALYSIS

- *At this point the discussion can go in any number of directions. You may want to begin by asking the group to choose one (or more) of the issues raised above as a focus by asking them which of the issues is most relevant to their practice. Or, as a facilitator, you may want to direct the conversation by choosing one (or more) of the issues raised and directing the discussion to meet your particular agenda for the group.*

- *For each of your discussion foci look at how that particular situation developed.*

  How do the players themselves (Alan, the case writer, the other participants) contribute to the situation?

  What do we know about this program and the people in it?

  What do we know about the educator? What role does she play in terms of choice of subject matter and responding to Alan in the past? Is this a new problem?

What role does Alan play in the group? For whom do you think he is speaking?

- *What did the family educator do, with what results, risks and consequences?*
- *How do you think the situation appeared to other participants and why do you think so? How do you understand the silence of the other participants?*

IV. INCORPORATING THE TEXT STUDY

- *How does our text study shed light on the case? (See "Large Group Discussion Point" #2.)*
- *Are there (other) Jewish value concepts that can help us see this issue from a Jewish perspective?* See the list of "Big Jewish Ideas" in the appendix. For example: *kavod, derech eretz, klal yisrael, mehila, tochecha*—how do they apply to our situation?

V. CASE EVALUATION

- *In your experience, is this situation typical?*
- *What might be other ways of handling this situation? What are the risks and benefits of each?*
- *Might their be a synagogue perspective that would come into play here?*
- *After our discussion would you refine your idea about what this is a case of?*
- *What lingering questions do you have?*

VI. CLOSURE–REFLECTION ON PRACTICE

Journaling and/or reflection in small groups is optional.

- *Choose a question that invites participants to connect the issues raised in the case discussion to their own practice of family education.*

For example: How could you prepare yourself for a discussion in which the topic of Christmas is likely to arise? How would the composition of the group affect your preparation? What other hot-button issues should you be prepared for?

- *Ask participants to extrapolate principles of practice–generalizations of good practice that could guide them in their own work.*
- *And/or have participants write about an issue from the case that was not discussed.*
- *And/or have participants reflect on the case study process: What new insights did you gain from our discussion? What part of the discussion did you find most challenging?*

CASE # 7 THE TALLIT PROJECT

Text: The Day Is Short

TEXT: *Pirkei Avot* (Ethics of the Fathers) 2:20-21 (Hebrew & English translation)

QUESTIONS FOR STUDY IN H̲EVRUTA

1) Look at 2:20—What types of work ("tasks") do you think this saying could apply to? Think of a minimum of three different kinds. Think through each part of the saying as you work out your three analogies:

   a) What is the "task"?   _____   _____   _____

   b) Who are the "workers?   _____   _____   _____

   c) What is the "reward"?   _____   _____   _____

   d) Who is the "master"?   _____   _____   _____

2) Look at 2:21—How do we strike a balance between the two parts of this saying? How do you, as a family educator, approach this challenge?

3) What do you make of the juxtaposition between this saying and the previous one?

LARGE GROUP DISCUSSION POINT—for the facilitator

Setting Limits. As family educators (and educators in general) we often feel overwhelmed. How do we begin to set limits? And in doing so, how do we respond to those who are not pleased by our saying "no"?

Text Study

The Day is Short: Pirkei Avot 2:20-21

[20]Rabbi Tarfon taught:

The day is short, the task is great, the workers are indolent, the reward bountiful, and the Master insistent (is knocking).

[21]He used to say: You are not obliged to finish the task, neither are you free to neglect it.

²⁰רַבִּי טַרְפוֹן אוֹמֵר:

הַיּוֹם קָצָר, וְהַמְּלָאכָה מְרֻבָּה,

וְהַפּוֹעֲלִים עֲצֵלִים, וְהַשָּׂכָר הַרְבֵּה,

וּבַעַל הַבַּיִת דּוֹחֵק.

²¹הוּא הָיָה אוֹמֵר:

לֹא עָלֶיךָ הַמְּלָאכָה לִגְמֹר

וְלֹא אַתָּה בֶן־חוֹרִין לִבָּטֵל מִמֶּנָּה.

Case #7: The Tallit Project

"I'm not sure I can commit that much time to this project," stated Alexandra as she reached for the rugelach (pastry). Two of the other mothers at the table nodded their agreement. "I have a *Bat Mitzvah* coming up in three months, and I'm really focused on that," Ariella added. The fourth parent, Evelyn, expressed an opposing viewpoint. "My son is really excited to be doing a family education project with Mrs. Goldman. He felt left out when he saw the children in her class working on that Jewish holiday project. He's really eager to work with his family on this *tallit*." Discussion continued back and forth across the table as to the pros and cons of embarking on a family education project when only eight weeks remained to the school year. Three of the four parents decided that three family sessions over a six-week period was too much to ask of them and the other families in the class.

I was perplexed by this discussion with my steering committee for the sixth-grade *tallit* project, because when my principal asked me in mid-March to take on the design and implementation of a family education project for Class 6A, I had been led to believe that there was strong "buy-in" for this program. I was new to my role as Director of Family Education for our K-8 Jewish community day school of 200 students. A lot of planning had gone into designing our new family education project and how we were going to introduce it to our community. In the original plan I was to pilot the program solely within my own sixth-grade class (6B). I was reluctant to do so.

I was somewhat uneasy about taking on a new project with a group of families I did not know well, and I really didn't have enough time to devote to yet another project, since I still had responsibility for teaching my own sixth-grade class. But being "a good soldier," I agreed to give it a go.

I had facilitated a successful family education project with my own class of thirteen families in the fall and had received generally positive feedback on both the process and product. Based on comments the principal heard from the parents in the other sixth-grade class—who were feeling left out of the family education loop—the principal had asked (pressured?) me to work with that class as well, so that all the sixth-grade families would have the opportunity to participate in family education. After consulting with several family education colleagues, I decided to offer a *tallit* project. I felt that the project was doable in the short time remaining in the school year and would be embraced by both the students and parents of 6A. Several of the 6A students had approached me over the course of the year to ask if I would be doing a project with their class. I was finally able to tell them what I was planning. They seemed delighted to have the opportunity to work together to create a *tallit* with their family members. I sent a letter home to the 6A parents, asking for volunteers for a steering committee and giving a basic outline of the project and its anticipated time commitment. I personally asked two parents whom I knew to serve on the committee. Both expressed interest and agreed to serve. Two other parents agreed to participate, and the first meeting was set for the beginning of April.

When it became clear that the time commitment was a major issue for three of the four parents on the steering committee, one mother asked whether there was another kind of project that could be done in a shorter time frame. I felt put upon by the group. I had (grudgingly) taken on the added responsibility of planning and implementing this project (in addition to my regular teaching duties with my own class) and had already spent a considerable amount of time researching and designing the program. I had sent out initial correspondence to the families two or three weeks prior to the steering committee meeting and had received no feedback during that period that indicated any misgivings by the parents. I really didn't feel that I could start over at this point to design a new program, and because I was a new family educator I could not easily and quickly reproduce something that had worked well in the past. In addition, I knew that the stakes were high due to the success of my project with Class 6B. A program of lesser scope and impressiveness would not be received kindly by the parents of 6A or by the school administration.

After hearing the committee members dispute the feasibility of embarking on the *tallit* project, I suggested that they poll the eleven other families in the class about their interest in moving ahead. I explained that for this particular project a minimum of two family gatherings would be necessary (although three would result in a far better process and product). The meeting ended on a conciliatory note, although I could not predict the eventual outcome. Evelyn, the last parent to leave the meeting, shared her disappointment with the attitude of the other parents on the committee. "After all," she said, "I'm probably the busiest parent in this group. I don't relish the idea of three gatherings either, but I know how much this means to my son, and I want him to participate in something Jewish with you as facilitator." I thanked her for her support and indicated that we'd have to await the consensus of the entire group. Evelyn predicted that the attitude of the committee members conducting the poll would bias the results. Sure enough, several days later they reported that only forty percent of the respondents supported the project. One parent even expressed outrage that I had told the students in the class that the project was going to take place prior to getting parent approval.

At this point, heading into the Passover season, I met with the principal to update him. After discussing the matter, we decided to abandon the project rather than try to force participation from parents who did not feel able to devote the time necessary to bring it to fruition. I reported back to my steering committee that it seemed best to discontinue the project at this time, and perhaps pick it up again the following year as a seventh-grade project, when the students were closer to their *Bat* and *Bar Mitzvah* and could create a *tallit* to wear at that *simcha*. There was some grumbling on the part of the parents that their children didn't get to participate in a family project, and they asked why the planning hadn't occurred early enough in the year to make it possible for both classes to have equal experiences. I was left feeling disenchanted and discouraged about the way the family education project ended its first year.

After reflecting on this experience, I wondered how I might have handled this process differently and formulated the following questions:

- Would it have been better to decline to conduct the *tallit* project entirely, given my own time constraints?
- Was it a good idea for a teacher unfamiliar with the students and families in a particular class to coordinate a family education project for that group?
- How could I have created more effective "buy-in" on the steering committee in this situation?
- What is the best model for organizing a new family education program in a day school?
- Should such a program begin in one class or grade level?
- Should teacher(s) within each grade level be responsible for implementing their own family education programs under the auspices of a director?

Commentary by Joan S. Kaye

Innovation of any sort creates excitement and risk. When the innovation includes a new population (families), the potential for both increases exponentially. The more people involved in the planning a new family education project, the better the chances of maximizing the former while minimizing the latter.

In this case, the plan seems to have been created solely by the new director of family education and the principal. It was apparently a plan for the entire school, beginning with a single project in the class taught by the director. The case states that "a lot of planning" went into how "we were going to introduce it to the community," meaning, I assume, with what program in what class or grade. The phrase "introduce it to the community" presents a problem in itself. Where was the community involvement in planning this major new program? How many parents were part of the process? How many of the faculty?

A commitment to a school-wide family education program is a commitment to change. It is fine to begin with a single pilot program, but the process of change involves much more than a single program. By hiring a director of family education, a statement is being made with far-reaching implications about the role of the school in the lives of the students and their entire families. It is essential that this statement be reflected in more than one classroom. If families are important, then they should participate in making decisions about programs that directly impact them. The atmosphere of the school should encourage parents to participate and make them feel welcome when they do so. (How are parents greeted when they enter the building? Are they encouraged to do so? Are there any materials on walls or display places for them to read and interact with? Is there a pot of coffee available or a place for them to sit if they want to hang around and chat in the morning? Are they welcome to visit classrooms? Are there clear guidelines for when they do visit?)

If families are important, all the teachers should be helped to find ways to involve parents in their work. Many, if not most, teachers neither know how to do this nor are comfortable doing it. They were trained to deal with children, and putting adults into the mix can be frightening as well as add more work to their load. Not involving them, however, runs two serious risks: First, family education will appear to be a series of programs, rather than a school commitment; and second, just like the parents in 6A, teachers will feel left out. If family education is seen as the new, glamorous program, and only one staff member is involved in its implementation, the rest of the staff may well resent both the program and that staff member. In this case, there is no mention of the teacher of 6A. Was her opinion ever sought? Did she have a relationship with the parents that could have helped the director avoid some of the problems she encountered? Often a teacher is left out of planning in a mistaken desire to save him or her extra work. While this is certainly a concern, the 6A teacher definitely has a stake in anything that involves the students in her classroom and should have at least a consultative role in the project.

Once a plan has been developed with representation from the parents and faculty, it should be presented to the affected community in a manner that demonstrates commitment not only to the project, but to including everyone in it. People need to understand that they will "have a turn," even though it might not be exactly when they would like it. Alternatively, they should be told that they will not get a turn (and the reasons why) and be given an opportunity to respond at a much earlier stage of the process. This obviously will not ensure that families will not feel left out when they see a successful program, but it provides a strong rationale for addressing their concerns in a less precipitate manner. I can only assume that there was good reason for the original plan's having only one project in its first year. At no point, apparently, were those reasons re-examined or discussed before the plan was changed. There is a fine line between being too rigid about sticking to a plan and being too willing to change it, but I would hope the original reasoning would be re-examined to determine whether a change is justified. One way to avoid having to change a plan in midstream is to present it so that everyone knows of its existence and its content at the outset.

If this plan was a major undertaking, it should have been presented with a big splash in a variety of ways. We don't know if the plan was ever distributed to the school population, but sending written notification of a major change is rarely sufficient. The writer's dismay at the parents' delayed response to what she had carefully laid out for them in writing graphically demonstrates the pitfalls in relying solely on written communication. Even when people read their mail, they don't always read it carefully, and until they are asked to act upon it, they don't realize its significance. It is wonderful that the professionals took the time to develop a K-8 plan rather than simply starting with a project, but the plan can be effective only when all those who are affected by it know about it and have bought into it.

The steering committee for the project is, unfortunately, a case of too little, too late. It is not exactly clear what their role is. Although the writer believed that the *tallit* project was doable and acceptable, feedback from the parents might have provided a more accurate view of what was "doable." Instead, the project was presented to the parents as a *fait accompli*. Could part of their negative reaction be ascribed to not having been consulted previously? After all, the letter the parents received informed them about a specific project; it did not consult them on their needs. Moreover, we do not know whether the letter actually requested feedback or the writer assumed that if people had negative reactions to the project, they would contact her. Once the steering committee rejected the initial idea, they were again left out of the process: The principal and teacher together decided to cancel the program and informed the committee about their decision. Again, the committee was left with no option other than to grumble at the decision that had been made for them, and all participants were left with negative feelings as a result of the experience.

For a new family educator, this kind of failure is particularly painful. As the writer realizes, the stakes are very high. The principal is applying pressure on one side; the parents on another; the students on a third—and, of course, there is her own strong desire to be successful in this new position. What supports does she need? First of all, there must be a clear job definition: What are the specific responsibilities of a director of family education? How do they fit with her pre-existing role as a sixth-grade classroom teacher? In a conflict, which has priority? If necessary, are there ways of relieving her from some classroom responsibilities during times of intensive family education work?

What does the family educator need from the principal? She feels that he is pressuring her to take on an added responsibility, and her reluctance to do so is clear. Could she possibly have negotiated another way out of the dilemma, one which wouldn't have left her feeling resentful? What is the responsibility of the family educator in this situation to ensure that she is not overburdened? If the principal doesn't do it, how can she take care of herself? When is it legitimate to say no, and how can professionals do so in a manner that protects their integrity without costing them their jobs?

The director of family education started the *tallit* project with many strikes against her: the lack of lay involvement at the beginning; her own attitude; the perceived need to do an impressive project (equal to one that had had much more planning and preparation time in the fall); and, finally, timing. It has been my experience that a similar phenomenon occurs with adults. The school year is winding down, and people seem to have an almost instinctive sense of their commitments for the remainder of the year. Trying to generate excitement about something new at this time is truly problematic, especially when that something new involves a significant commitment of previously unbudgeted time on the part of both the participants and the professional. It seems that the problem here was not with the focus of the project, but with the amount of time it would take and the time of year. Perhaps the educator's time would have been better spent in researching two or three projects of varying scope and presenting them to the parents to choose among, rather than fully developing a single idea before bringing it to the group. It is not so much that she didn't have an adequate repertoire to make a quick switch, but that the time she used in developing the *tallit* project would have been better used in finding two or three different projects and getting a first-hand sense of the group (rather than only the principal's opinion) before developing any of them.

Most of this analysis is concerned with what could have been done to prevent the writer's negative experience. What might have been done to rescue it, once the disaster had occurred? After the parents objected to the commitment required for the initial project, what could have been done to end the year on a positive note for the parents, children and professionals? Involving the parents in the decision to cancel the *tallit* project could have provided an opportunity for them to define the parameters for a project they would like to do in the following year; perhaps there could have been a similar conversation with the children as well. Rather than an announcement of an aborted project and an occasion for grumbling, that final meeting could have been turned into the beginning of a planning process for the following year. Another possibility might have been to rework the *tallit* project to begin that spring and continue into the *b'nai mitzvah* year the following fall. That way, the parents and children could have had some activities together with a smaller investment of time, and the year would have ended on a happier note for all concerned.

Commentary by Marian Gribetz

Although this case involves family education in a day school setting, we can certainly learn a lot from it that can be translated to other settings, such as congregational schools and JCCs. After all, in all settings we are after the same result, stronger Jewish families that can create meaningful Jewish lives in the community. Some of the issues that I see in this case are explored below.

Lead time. Lead time is needed to get parents to commit to projects in the school. Parents are often asked to, and feel compelled to, devote a lot of time to their children's education. Projects come home that need help from parents, whether it's buying materials, going to the library or generally being available to help with homework. Asking parents, especially of sixth-graders—when new adolescent/parent relationships are beginning—to attend sessions together with their children without appropriate lead time and "buy-in" can be a setup for dissension and discontent, as was evident in this scenario.

Good communication. Good communication to the families at every step creates a good climate for participation and cooperation. When a project is launched for a school at the beginning of the year (or even at the end of the previous year when plans are being made), good communication to the school community is a necessity. If we look at this case as an example of any educational change, it becomes apparent that many constituencies should be informed and consulted throughout the process. Educators often lament the lack of interaction, as does the teacher in this case with respect to the lack of parental feedback indicating misgivings in response to her letter to the parents. The teacher fails to recognize that she had missed an opportunity to create a conversation with the parents; her letter was a one-way flow of information.

Educators must respect the pressures that parents face week in and week out. In our classrooms we respect and acknowledge students who learn and respond in different ways. A teacher would not conclude that a student "failed" just because he or she had not responded to the sole piece of information that was transmitted about a particular topic. We should likewise recognize that parents (whom we now want to embrace as students) also have multiple forces bombarding them daily.

Including the community. Include your community during the planning stages. Don't just assume that because a few professionals think you have a good idea (and maybe you've even received funding from your community), everyone's expectations are the same. In this case, it seems that the principal and the director of family education came together to plan the pilot for one particular class, and when that pilot succeeded, others began murmuring that they wanted in, too.

Early communication from the principal to the community about the nature of the pilot was needed. Planning should involve other members of the community beyond the professionals, and communication about this planning process should be the responsibility of all the planners so that there will be many informed and invested advocates for the project.

The content of the project. The content of the family education project should resonate with the families. When she proposed the *tallit* project for the end of the sixth grade, the teacher hoped the families would see it as a powerful project to complete before the *bar/bat mitzvah* year. The responses of parents on the steering committee and to the survey showed otherwise. The steering committee meeting (and any other dialogue with parents) could have been a "teachable moment" at which the parents might have learned to see past their own busy schedules to the potential power of the project and its appropriateness to the end of sixth grade.

The alternate idea–doing the *tallit* project the following year, closer to the *bar/bat mitzvah*–has some appeal. Connecting the project to the *bar/bat mitzvah*, and promoting it as connected to the students' preparation for this milestone, is likely to strengthen the parents' motivation to be involved with the project. However, even if the project is implemented the following year, lots of advance preparation is needed. The family educator and others involved should be informed of and sensitive to the life cycles of these families. There are probably those whose *b'nai mitzvah* will occur after the seventh grade, so it would also be important to pay attention to the scheduled dates of the children's *b'nai mitzvah*.

Polls and surveys. Be cautious about conducting polls and surveys; review available information first. While it is certainly of utmost importance to understand the needs and desires of the families with whom you will be working, surveying people about their opinions of specific programmatic ideas may be a mistake. In our case the attitude of the steering committee members may well have influenced the results. When we do ask people for their input, we must be careful about what we are really asking them and what impact the results of our questioning will have.

Educators often have access to lots of information about the families with whom they work that will help to make informed decisions about programs. Before jumping to conducting polls, we should review the information we already have.

For example, we probably know: how many children most of our students' families have; whether more than one child is in the school; the children's ages and birth order; whether both parents are working; whether the parents are active in other areas of the school and community life; the families' neighborhoods; and the like. Surveys that ask more questions or the same questions may set up the wrong expectations. Use the information you already have and then figure out what else you need to know. You may only need to ask *one* question, to poll a few representative families instead of surveying the entire community.

Desired outcomes, big questions, criteria for success. Think about your desired outcomes, articulate the big questions and generate criteria for success. When we set out to create new ways of educating (like family education), we should be clear about our desired outcomes and ready for some possible surprise outcomes. In this case, it is unclear what the principal's desired outcome was, but I assume that, if nothing else, it was generating interest in having more family education programs in the school. If some possible outcomes are articulated prior to the pilot program, there will be a better climate for anticipating the next steps when the desired outcomes are achieved or when surprise outcomes happen. Here, the pilot program had a great outcome and should have been the foundation for future programs.

So what went wrong? What should have happened to build on the success of the pilot? Was the teacher pressured to pull off a second "pilot" with the second class without the time and support needed for her to do so?

Educators constantly make decisions on their feet. When we see students eager to continue exploring a subject, we decide to allow that to happen or to table the subject and continue with our planned activities. Many forces play into those decisions. In the case of family education, those forces also include the wishes of the families in the second class, the time constraints of pulling off a program on short notice and how much the delivery system can withstand. Together the principal and director of family education could have thought through the presenting problems creatively and come up with a few possible solutions before even opening up the discussion to the steering committee.

Revisit goals and objectives. Finally, think about goals and objective and be open to revisiting them. It is important in the development of family education in institutions to engage in open, active and reflective conversation about goals and objectives, which can lead to "buy-in" by all the affected parties. Whether or not the classroom teacher, as opposed to a "family education specialist," is the one who implements the program is less important than ensuring that the classroom teacher is involved in the process. The actual deployment of personnel depends on the schedule of the institution as well as the particular interests and professional strengths of the teachers.

Annotated Lesson Plan
(Notes for the Facilitator)

I.   CASE OVERVIEW

   - *Facilitator's Summary:* The Director of Family Education in a Jewish Community Day School was led to believe that there was strong buy-in for a *tallit*-making program for 6th graders and their parents. However, late in the year, parents on a steering committee decided that the time commitment was too much for families. The project was abandoned. The educator struggles with her role in the undoing of this project

   - *Help the group determine what facts will be most useful in really understanding this case. It may be helpful to list them on the board.*

II. "WHAT IS THIS A CASE OF?"

   In the groups with which we have studied this case, participants raised issues such as:

   - Managing workload and the inability to say "no"
   - Working with committees
   - Dealing with multiple pressures
   - Planning
   - Knowing your audience
   - Getting "buy-in"
   - Program implementation and role division
   - *Kol hatchalot kashot*—all beginnings (new projects) are difficult (at first)
   - Lack of communication

   Your group may come up with different or additional issues.

III. CASE ANALYSIS

   - *At this point the discussion can go in any number of directions. You may want to begin by asking the group to choose one (or more) of the issues raised above as a focus by asking them which of the issues is most relevant to their practice. Or, as a facilitator, you may want to direct the conversation by choosing one (or more) of the issues raised and directing the discussion to meet your particular agenda for the group.*

   - *For each of your discussion foci look at how that particular situation developed.*

     How do the players themselves (the principal, the parents, the writer) contribute to the situation?

     What do we know about this program?

     What do we know about the educator? What is her attitude toward the program? What is her attitude toward the steering committee and other parents?

   - *How do you think the situation appeared to the families and why do you think so?*

   - *What did the family educator do, with what results, risks and consequences?*

IV. INCORPORATING THE TEXT STUDY

- *How does our text study shed light on the case?* (See "Large Group Discussion Point" #1.)
- *Are there (other) Jewish value concepts that can help us see this issue from a Jewish perspective?* See the list of "Big Jewish Ideas" in the appendix. For example: *kavvana*—how does it apply to our situation?

V. CASE EVALUATION

- *In your experience, is this situation typical?*
- *What might be other ways of handling this situation? What are the risks and benefits of each?*
- *After our discussion would you refine your idea about what this is a case of?*
- *What lingering questions do you have?*

VI. CLOSURE—REFLECTION ON PRACTICE

Journaling and/or reflection in small groups is optional.

- *Choose a question that invites participants to connect the issues raised in the case discussion to their own practice of family education.*

    For example: How have you dealt with pressure from parents (or groups of parents)? What boundaries do you set for yourself?

- *Ask participants to extrapolate principles of practice—generalizations of good practice that could guide them in their own work.*
- *And/or have participants write about an issue from the case that was not discussed.*
- *And/or have participants reflect on the case study process: What new insights did you gain from our discussion? What part of the discussion did you find most challenging?*

CASE #8 "DINNER ON SHABBAT OR SHABBAT DINNER?"

Text: Oneg Shabbat

TEXTS: Pesikta Rabbati 23:16 and excerpt from Abraham Joshua Heschel,
The Sabbath

QUESTIONS FOR STUDY IN <u>HEVRUTA</u>

1) What traditional tension about the purpose of Shabbat is revealed in Pesikta Rabbati?

2) As a "professional Jew" would your ideal Shabbat be with the "workers" or the "scholars"?

3) Can you find additional ways of harmonizing the two opinions presented in Pesikta Rabbati?

4) According to Heschel, what is the purpose of Shabbat, and what is its source?

5) What does he offer to counterbalance his concerns about people?

6) How does Heschel's position comment on the previous text?

LARGE GROUP DISCUSSION POINTS—for the facilitator

What is Shabbat?

Try to define the key elements of Shabbat. What elements do you think have the ability to excite families? What is the educator's role in bringing these elements to families? Is Shabbat always the best place to start off with families? What are some of the potential problems with teaching Shabbat as a curricular piece in family education?

Text Study

I. Pesikta Rabbati 23:16

[ר' ברכיה בשם] ר' חייא [בר אבא] לא ניתנה השבת אלא לתענוג.
רבי חגי בשם רבי שמואל בר נחמן לא ניתנה השבת
אלא לתלמוד תורה
ולא פליגי, (מאן) [מה] דאמר רבי ברכיה בשם רבי חייא בר אבא
לתענוג.
אלו תלמידי חכמים שהם יגיעים בתורה כל ימות השבת
ובשבת הם באים ומענגים.
מה דאמר רבי חגי בשם רבי שמואל בר נחמן לתלמוד תורה.
אילו הפועלים שהם עסוקים במלאבתן, של ימות השבת
ובשבת הם באים ומתעסקים בתורה.

Rabbi Hiyya ben Abba: The Shabbat was given for enjoyment. Rabbi Shmuel ben Nahmani: The Shabbat was given for studying Torah.

One saying does not contradict the other. Rabbi Hiyya was speaking about scholars who spend the week studying Torah and use Shabbat to enjoy themselves. Rabbi Shmuel was talking about workers who are busy with their work all week, and on Shabbat they come and study Torah.

II. Abraham Joshua Heschel, *The Sabbath*

The Sabbath is the most precious present mankind has received from the treasure house of God. All week we think: The spirit is too far away, and we succumb to spiritual absenteeism, or at best we pray: Send us a little of Thy spirit. On the Sabbath the spirit stands and pleads: Accept all excellence from me… Yet what the spirit offers is often too august for our trivial minds. We accept the ease and relief and miss the inspirations of the day, where it comes from and what it stands for. This is why we pray for understanding: "May Thy children realize and understand that their rest comes from Thee, and that to rest means to sanctify Thy name."

(From the afternoon prayer on Shabbat, page 18)

Case #8 " Dinner on Shabbat or Shabbat Dinner?"

The congregation gradually assembled in the sanctuary as the Erev Shabbat Family service progressed. Some congregants came in with prayer books; some didn't. Some opened the books; others participated from memory. Still others just sat quietly and patiently, waiting for the service to conclude. It struck me that few if any people were actually participating in the *davenning*. There were more visitors than usual, which seemed to me to make the service even more spiritless. Even the storyteller we had brought in to add a little uplift to the service didn't seem to be "on."

At the end of the service congregants greeted each other and slowly made their way to the social hall for the *shabbat* dinner, talking and catching up. When everyone finally arrived in the social hall they were asked to sit at tables, by families, so that the *Shabbat* table rituals could be conducted. After a good bit of encouragement everyone found a seat. Some sat as families, although many, especially pre-teens and teens and their parents, sat with their peers.

Once everyone finally became quiet, the blessings for the candles, for children, the *Kiddush* and the *Motzi* were done. It was hard to maintain the focus of the group. A collective sigh of relief was almost audible when all the blessings were completed and it was finally time to begin eating dinner. The stampede to the buffet began, and any remaining semblance of *shabbat* immediately vanished.

Within ten minutes of sitting down to eat, everyone under ten years old finished, got up from the table and was off to a nearby room to run around, play and hang out. I watched many of the parents who were still at the tables continue to eat at a relatively leisurely pace and carry on conversations with the other adults they were sitting with. They were enjoying themselves and seemed very comfortable with what was happening.

After a while the children were asked to come back into the social hall to hear the storyteller complete the story he had started during services. Next we tried to sing some *shabbat* songs. Songbooks were passed out, but the same low level of participation that had characterized the service continued during the singing. Either people didn't know the songs or they just were not in the mood to sing. I tried short songs, songs by request and some songs that many people knew. After seeing that most people did not join in the first few songs, I gave up and announced what at least all the kids were waiting for—dessert. After eating dessert, families gradually began to clean up and go home. I felt relieved, though sad, that it was all finally over.

Except for the guests, most of the eighty people who attended this service and dinner were regular participants in this semi-monthly event. There are usually equal numbers of adults and children, the majority of whom are seven years old or younger. Over the past ten years the numbers attending these dinners, which are no-charge potluck dairy dinners at which the synagogue provides a hot entree, has gradually increased, and now sixty to ninety people attend each time. Interest has grown to the point that sometimes we even have to cut off registration. Some families have been coming since the beginning, but generally families cycle into the mix when their kids are very young and cycle out at about the time they become teenagers.

This family service and dinner is only one element of a very extensive family education program at our synagogue. We have ongoing activities and programs for families with children of all ages, including a series of Sunday morning pre-kindergarten family activities, a family school program modeled after Family Room,[1] occasional teen/parent workshops, monthly Friday Night Tot Shabbat services, as well as family-oriented holiday activities.

Until a year ago, the family *shabbat* service and dinner was held monthly, but then I decided to schedule it every other month for two reasons:

First, the dinners were a monthly disappointment to me. As discussed below, my hopes and expectations for them were not being fulfilled. Second, my real goal in organizing these programs was to encourage people to "do" *shabbat* at home. As a result of thinking through this goal, I decided to start a new program called *Shabbat-to-Go* (which takes place during the alternate months when we do not have a dinner). *Shabbat-to-Go* begins with an early Friday night service, after which people go to one another's homes for *shabbat* dinner and the evening. The goal is not to teach home ritual or have family education during the service, but to stimulate people to invite each other to their homes for *shabbat*. Judging by the number of participants, *Shabbat-to-Go* has met with very limited success to date.

Through the years, the large *shabbat* evening dinners, which seem to be meaningful for the families attending, have been less than successful from my perspective. It's obvious (from the ongoing attendance of the same families) that the social and community-building needs of these adults and children are being met. My guess would be that, if asked, these families would respond that their "Jewish" needs are also being met. Yet from my viewpoint, the evenings are not and rarely have been "successful" Jewishly.

The sense of *shabbat* that I would like the families to experience during the evening and to carry home afterwards doesn't appear to be there. I don't believe that they would want to transfer from the synagogue to their homes the kind of *shabbat* experience these particular dinners provide. There's plenty of *ruach* (spirit) during the evening—lots of energy and interaction during the dinner—but little of the traditional *ruach shabbat* (spirit of Shabbat), i.e., leisurely eating, singing and discussions with Jewish content. The dinner is just that: a dinner taking place on *shabbat*, devoid of that intangible quality that would make it a *shabbat* dinner for me. Consequently,

---

[1] Vicky Kelman, *Family Room: Linking Families into a Jewish Learning Community*, The Shirley and Arthur Whizin Institute for Jewish Family Life of the University of Judaism (Los Angeles), 1995.

these programs have become a source of frustration, and often a demoralizing one, for me.

These realizations and this reality make me wonder about a number of issues:

Are there ways to enhance the Jewish content and process of the evening without scaring people away?

Is the family service and dinner the appropriate vehicle to accomplish my goal?

What can I do to increase the likelihood that these dinners will be successful from my perspective?

Should I be more assertive in trying to keep the families together throughout the whole evening? Would this create a more positive *shabbat* experience for me and for them?

What is the risk of trying to change a popular program? What are the tradeoffs?

Might change negatively impact the community-building that now occurs during these evenings? If yes, how?

Should I accept and be content with knowing that these evenings are no more than successful community-building activities?

Commentary by Ron Wolfson

"Shabbat Shalom!" In my thirty years in the field of Jewish education, these are the two words that have resonated most with me. They are, in fact, among the first words I can remember learning in my own family, although truth be told, it was probably *"Gut Shabbes!"* Of all the holiday celebrations we try to foster in Jewish family education, *shabbat*, especially the Friday night dinner experience, is perhaps the most challenging and potentially rewarding.

The obvious first question raised by this case is one that my colleagues and I have often discussed—and disagreed about the point: "Is *shabbat* the best place to start with Jewish family education?" If you could begin your work in family education by choosing one holiday celebration, would it be *shabbat*? On the one hand, *shabbat* is arguably the most important holiday. If you can encourage families to take *shabbat* seriously, they are much more likely to take on the other holidays. After all, *shabbat* offers the family a regularly scheduled Jewish time each week. On the other hand, *shabbat* is much more complicated than almost any other Jewish celebration. Wouldn't it be wiser to start with something simpler—Hanukkah, Purim, even Passover?

When I was approached to begin work on what became *The Art of Jewish Living* series of materials,[1] this was exactly the question presented to me. I chose to begin the series with "The Shabbat Seder" because I believed then, as I believe now, that no matter how difficult the challenge, empowering families to celebrate *shabbat* on a weekly basis can fundamentally change the Jewish character of the family system, strengthen the "familyness" of the family, and lead families into broader and deeper Jewish practice. I believe the place to begin is precisely the Friday night dinner celebration, for the following reasons:

• Dinner is the meal that is most regularly attended by family members;

• Friday night is the end of the week—a time when many families are predisposed to eat together;

• Welcoming the *shabbat* by marking its beginning is much easier than "checking in" at some other time during the day;

• The traditional *shabbat* dinner contains important building blocks for Jewish identity and continuity.

Nevertheless—and this directly bears on the issues presented in our case—Friday night can be the worst time of the week for families to sit together at a formal meal. Everyone is wired and tired from a long week of school and work. The last thing many families

---

[1] Ron Wolfson, *The Art of Jewish Living*, a series of books on the celebration of Jewish holidays in the home, sponsored by the Federation of Jewish Men's Clubs (New York) and the University of Judaism (Los Angeles). Books in the series include *The Art of Jewish Living: The Shabbat Seder*, 1985; *The Art of Jewish Living: Hannukah*, 1988/1990; *The Art of Jewish Living: The Passover Seder*, 1988 (translated into Russian, 1990); and *A Time to Mourn, A Time to Comfort*, 1993.

want to do is get dressed up and go to the synagogue, or the table, for a fancy dinner. Most people are ready to crash, looking forward to a relaxing weekend. Young children and their carpooling parents are especially worn out.

Yet the popularity of family Friday night dinners cannot be disputed. Most schools and synagogues schedule these events regularly, often once a year for each grade level. They are a staple of Jewish family education programming. But, as the author of our case frankly admits, they often fail to meet the expectations of both the families and the educators who sponsor them. As someone who has led Friday night *shabbat* "*seders*" in many institutions over the years, I can comment directly on the case as presented and can raise some questions that highlight broader principles of Jewish family education practice.

The case presents the typical Friday night scenario in a congregation. The evening begins with a "family service"–often a substitute for the "regular" Friday evening *Kabbalat Shabbat* service. Beginning with a service can be a stimulating start to a great event *if* the service itself is stimulating. More often than not, however, the service is merely a rehash of the tired regular worship, not an experience specifically designed for families. To the credit of the educator in our case, at least an attempt was made to bring in a fresh voice–a storyteller–to engage the families and young children. Yet even this effort seems to have been swallowed up by the spiritless service. If the evening must begin with a service, we should attempt to create a worship experience specifically tailored for families with little or no access to the regular prayer service. We can do so by emphasizing prayers that are familiar, at least to the children, and music that is familiar or, at the very least, repeatable–for example, *niggunim* (wordless melodies). Where is the service held? If fewer than one hundred souls rattle around in a huge sanctuary, no sense of community can be built. If the cantor sings *at* the congregation, rather than *with* it, no spirit will develop. If the rabbi delivers a standard sermon, many will be asleep before the evening has begun. Think of gathering the group in a smaller chapel, of adding popular and well-known songs to the service, and of forgoing sermons, even stories, in favor of buying time for the experience and celebration to follow.

The case correctly points to a major decision for the family educator to make, even before the families enter the room for dinner: where to seat them. Clearly, older children and teens often want to sit with each other, not with their parents. But what is the message we send when we allow them to do so? If one of the purposes of the family dinner is for the family to celebrate together, it is not sufficient to simply have family members in same room. The kids will find each other soon enough–usually about ten minutes after the food is served. For the main ritual part of the evening, families should be seated together.

The "feeling tone" of the evening is set at the dining hall door. Are there "greeters" to welcome the families with a warm "*Shabbat Shalom*"? Is the room attractive? Are there centerpieces on the tables? Is there a *shabbat* "goody bag" for each family to use at the table and/or to take home? Does the room look, feel and smell like *shabbat*? People pay attention to detail; recruit a lay committee and challenge the members to make the evening as attractive as any dinner party they would host in their own homes.

The next question is the central issue presented in the case: What is the purpose of bringing the families together for *shabbat* dinner? If the purpose is socializing, that clearly happens among the families in our case. But if the purpose is to have these families experience a *shabbat* celebration and learn how to "do it" at home, a number of questions must be addressed.

First, are written texts provided to the participants? Most participants in family education events do not know the rituals or the words of the rituals by heart. Having the rabbi, cantor or educator stand in front of the assembly and "perform" the blessings while everyone else looks around at each other is, it seems to me, a wasted educational opportunity. Families should have access to a carefully assembled text of the blessings for the *shabbat* table, with Hebrew, English transliteration and English translation (and Russian, if there are recent immigrants from the former Soviet Union). These texts ought to be available for the participants to take home at the conclusion of the evening.

Second, are there ritual objects on each table? It is not enough to have one ceremonial table at the front of the room, especially if the room is a large auditorium. If the evening is to model what might happen at home, each table should have on it candlesticks, *kiddush* cups, *hallot* and a *challah* cover, and flowers or some sort of centerpiece. Even if the official candle lighting time has long since passed when the families sit down at the table, having candlesticks on each table presents an image of what a family table ought to look like. (Have the candles lit before the dinner or pretend to light them when practicing the candle blessing.)

Third, is there a leader? As in any good *seder*, there should be a designated person to lead the families through the major steps of the celebration, explain the meaning of each step briefly, and provide precise instructions about how to practice the ritual. Let's take the blessing of the children as an example. The leader can direct attention to the text of the blessings, explain why we hope our daughters will be "like Sarah, Rebecca, Rachel and Leah" and our sons "like Ephraim and Menassheh," and ask questions, such as What is there about the sons of Joseph that merits their inclusion in this blessing? or Why do the parents, and not the rabbi, recite the "priestly" benediction over the children? The leader can then suggest that parents not pronounce the blessing in a formal manner, but encourage the kids to climb into their laps to receive this blessing. To get parents to do this requires a genuinely enthusiastic attitude and even a bit of *chutzpah* on the leader's part. Readiness on the part of the participants to try the ritual depends to a large degree on the leader's encouragement and enthusiasm. Explain, demonstrate, encourage—these are the bywords of a good teacher of ritual.

The author of the case study laments that it was difficult to get everyone quiet and focused. Remember, everyone is tired, wired and hungry. Unless the ritual is presented in an interesting way, families will treat it as the obstacle standing between them and dinner. On the other hand, an entertaining, interesting and well-paced interactive demonstration of the entire ritual can capture their interest and participation. Ask everyone to do and say everything–for the sake of education. Ask everyone to join hands or to stand and put arms around shoulders and sway to the singing of "*Shalom Aleichem.*" This alone can help build the kind of *ruach* that can pervade the evening.

Lest one think that this learner's *Shabbat Seder* takes forever, it has been my experience that candle lighting, *Shalom Aleichem*, blessing the children, *Kiddush*, hand washing, and *ha-Motzi* can be taught and performed in twenty to twenty-five minutes. As for the hunger, remember that, if the evening began at 6:00 p.m. with an hour-long service, it is likely to be 7:30 before anything of substance is available to eat. Put platters of carrot sticks or crackers on each table to nibble on while the ritual is explained and performed.

It is true that once dinner is served, the children and teenagers will split. Fine–that's what happens in my house, too. The important thing in the institutional setting is not to let the kids run wild. Have a baby-sitter for the youngest children and a teacher willing to work with the elementary age kids. This enables parents to sit guilt-free and socialize with their friends: Nothing wrong with that.

Another challenge is to refocus the group when it comes time for *zemirot* (Shabbat songs) and creating the kind of *shabbat ruach* everyone hopes for. Some strategies that work to get everyone's attention: Have the kids prepare a skit while with the teacher and then perform it; have a storyteller (as in our case); get a fabulous song leader who knows how to work with a Friday night crowd of families. Choose songs that everyone knows. Camp songs with interactive parts and hand motions work best: "*David Melekh Yisrael*," "*V'aineinu Tirena*," "*Shabbat Shalom,* Hey!" or "Gilly Gilly Gilly Gilly Good *Shabbat*," etc. Have a "*Hiney Ma Tov*" sing-down: Ask the adults, many of whom were Jewish summer campers, to recall their favorite tune. Build the *ruach*, get a group dancing, and the evening will fly. Then, over dessert, have family discussion time at the *shabbat* table. Have the youngest person ask everyone seated at the table a question, such as "What was your favorite time this past week?" Encourage the families to talk with each other over dessert and conclude the event with *Birkat HaMazon*. And don't drag out the evening. Families with young children want to be on their way home before 9:00 p.m.

One of the central questions to ask about any Jewish family education event is: "What goes home?" If the teaching and the experience during the event itself has been effective, the families will take home a model of what they can do in their own homes. But that is often not enough to sustain Jewish practice in the long run. Families need what Vicky Kelman calls "scaffolding"–materials and support that can help the family build its expertise.[2] Think of having a "goody bag" for each family to take home from the *shabbat* dinner experience: the texts of the blessings; explanations and directions for the rituals; an audiotape of chants of the blessings and *zemirot* (Shabbat songs);

[2]Vicky Kelman, *Jewish Family Retreats: A Handbook,* The Melton Research Center of The Jewish Theological Seminary of America (New York) and The Shirley and Arthur Whizin Institute of the University of Judaism (Los Angeles), 1992, p. 11

family discussion questions; *shabbat* celebration ideas; *shabbat* stories; even ideas for projects to make at home, such as a *challah* cover or a *kiddush* cup.

The author of our case has the right idea about encouraging families to join together in their own homes to support one another's learning and experience of *shabbat*. This goal, however, requires excellent organization and lots and lots of encouragement. Personal hospitality is a lost art in our generation. Make it easier by suggesting potluck dinners, having a come-as-you-are dress code, and inviting several families instead of just one (which can often be uncomfortable if the chemistry between the two families is not just right.). Another way to follow up the evening is to offer a short-term workshop on the skills of *shabbat* celebration in the weeks after the event. You may not attract a big crowd, but remember, Jewish families are made one at a time.

In my experience, the audience for institutional *shabbat* dinners is a mixed bag. Although some families are novices at Jewish celebration, many families who attend the family Friday night dinners already "do *shabbat*" at home. Why? They come to these events for various reasons: They don't have to cook; they also enjoy socializing with other families in the congregation or school—an important part of any successful community-building event; the "grandparents" in the congregation really look forward to these evenings—with or without their own grandchildren in attendance.

The author's last question is whether he should be content with knowing that these evenings are "no more than successful community-building activities." My answer is that he should know and accept that community-building is no mean accomplishment. But he should not settle for only that. I am convinced that a well-planned and executed family *shabbat* dinner can offer participants a superior experience of *shabbat* and give them the skills and encouragement to try it at home. Take advantage of the families' interest and willingness to sign up for these popular events to build an evening that is experiential, educational, entertaining and encouraging.

Commentary by Stuart Seltzer

The principal goal of the *Erev Shabbat* family programs described in this case was to enable and encourage congregational families to have authentic Friday night *shabbat* celebrations in their own homes. According to the author, while the family programs he instituted were popular, they failed to meet this goal in two respects: First, it seems that few families have transferred to their homes the experiences they had at the group dinners. Second, the institutional dinners lack, in his view, the kind of traditional *ruach shabbat* he had hoped to instill.

What, if anything, could this educator have done to better achieve his goal and to have the people gathered in the social hall experience that traditional *shabbat* feeling? I suggest that a table-centered dinner program, such as the one presented below, could better approximate an authentic family *shabbat* experience. After several table-centered dinners have occurred, a next step may be to have families actually go back to someone's house after the group service, rather than eat in the synagogue.

In the program described in the case, the participants came to the synagogue right after work, and then worshiped as a large group. If there had been no institutional group dinner, we hope that they would return home after the service for an intimate *shabbat* dinner gathering. In my view, the spirit of *shabbat* comes from the ritual and the roles people play around the dinner table. To impart the feeling generated at a traditional *shabbat* meal, we should make the individual table, rather than the room as a whole, the basic unit of the dinner celebration.

I myself was led toward Judaism by experiencing *shabbat* at the home of a family whom I will call the Levines—a couple with three children. The Levine family and their guests all enjoyed the meal and the whole experience around the table. No one had to be told to turn off the TV and come to the table. We waited to be called. *Shabbat* is about enjoyment—of the food, of each other, of the prescribed ritual, and of the rituals the family has invented. I enjoyed the fact that each person had his or her favorite food and knew that it would be served on *shabbat*. I enjoyed the way the conversation included everyone and everything, from the serious to the lighthearted, so that everyone could participate. The Levine family was prepared for this time of special conversation, anticipating it as they did their favorite foods. I enjoyed the way everyone had a role to play in the formal ritual: One recited the *Kiddush*, another led the *Birkat HaMazon*. I especially enjoyed one ritual that the Levine family had created. Mr. Levine threw the bread across the table to each person. (*Shabbat* dinner became an athletic contest.) The first time I was there, I asked myself, Is this holy? Are we allowed to toss bread? But I eventually decided that I wouldn't want to be part of a *shabbat* ceremony where this kind of fun was prohibited. There was also singing and study. After the meal, Mrs. Levine opened a special drawer—closed at all other times—where she had hidden special *shabbat* treats.

Even in a large room where people don't know each other or the ritual that well, it is possible to re-create the kind of *shabbat* feeling that characterized the Levine home by including many of the elements described in my example: an emphasis on enjoyment; intimacy; anticipation of the gathering and of the formal and personal rituals; giving everyone a role to play; valuing each person's likes and dislikes; inventing new *shabbat* customs; permitting participants to choose the roles in which they are most comfortable; and the general philosophy that the way to the holy was through the ordinary—food, conversation, fun and song. The role of the family educator is to recognize the importance of all these elements of the family *shabbat* table experience and to empower the participants at each table to experience them.

In this table-centered model, the *shabbat* rituals are performed, as much as possible, by each table for itself. After singing *Shalom Aleichem* as a large group, the leader should facilitate a transition by saying, for example, "This is the last time before the very end of the evening that I am going to speak to you as a large group, because tonight each table will represent a dining room table in a home where family and friends have gathered for *shabbat* dinner. Now you will begin your own *shabbat* dinners. And, if you permit me, I would like to listen in and see how you are celebrating *shabbat*."

Instead of having a storyteller tell a story to the whole room, which may distance the participants from their individual tables, the family educator can ask questions or suggest discussion topics—new ones each month, such as: What is the first *shabbat* you remember? Why did it make an impression? Through discussing these questions, the participants become their own storytellers.

To make this table-centered model succeed, the family educator may have to make some arrangements in advance. For example, seating at the tables can be assigned based on pre-existing friendships, and participants can be informed in advance of their dinner companions. Placecards can be set up on each table with family names. A *mezuzah* can also be placed on each table to emphasize that each table is in a home. The educator might choose a leader for each table and briefly orient him or her to the leader's role. Someone might be assigned to lead and explain the Friday night *kiddush*. Someone might be asked to personalize the ritual for blessing the *challah*. One person at each table can be asked in advance to bring an object that has a story behind it, such as a plate or a *kiddush* cup, to share with their table.

Ritual roles can be assigned or taught in advance. The family educator might offer learning sessions during the week prior to the dinner for people who want to learn about the rituals before the event. People who learn and then find something personally meaningful can then share it with the group at the dinner. One parent I know learned how to bless the candles and connected personally with the tradition of covering one's eyes and then seeing the flame. Her son asked, "Mommy, why do you cover your eyes so long?" She explained, "I like to be in the darkness for a while before looking in the light again." These personal explanations and connections can inspire others to experiment with the ritual. The more families experience these kinds of individual experiences and thoughts, the more each table will be able to function as an independent unit.

Not everything is going to be meaningful for everyone. I didn't come to the *shabbat* ritual at the Levines' as someone filled with faith. The ritual brought me a sanctified feeling. One of the important benefits of *shabbat* is the enjoyment of the end of a productive week and the pause before the challenges of the coming week. On *shabbat* we emphasize this enjoyment.

The family educator should not expect holiness, but should foster enjoyment, participation and intimacy, which can lead to holiness. The role of the educator is to seize upon what is positive in the room and build on it. For example, in the case study, the intimate conversation at the tables was a positive thing. The educator might say, "It is so nice to hear the noise in this room. After a long day at work, at school, at home, we can come together and talk." Toward the end of the meal the educator might say, "Let's change the noise for a few minutes. On your table is a poem. Read it aloud to yourselves, responsively. What does it mean to you, to all of us sitting around the table? Share your ideas. I am interested in what you think." Then the educator might go around the room and listen and respond to the conversations. This requires the educator to understand that not everybody is going to talk and to let each person find his or her role at the table. The educator keeps going from table to table until he finds something fun for everyone. At one table the family educator might say, "Let me teach you a song." At another table he might ask: "How did you pass the bread? Who said the blessing at your tale? Did anything funny happen? Did the table seem to come up with a theme or a way of doing things? Did someone become the leader?"

At the end of the meal the educator might get back to the large group by having volunteers report on what they most enjoyed about the meal or what each table did.

The family educator is not dictating what happens at each table or even expecting anything in particular. He is interested in what happened and may try to relate it in some small way to the spirit of *shabbat*. He makes some suggestions, and he allows the people to make him a *shabbat* guest at their tables. Maybe the measure of success for a program like this is not how you host it, but how you become a gracious guest.

Annotated Lesson Plan
(Notes for the Facilitator)

I. CASE OVERVIEW
- *Facilitator's Summary:* A synagogue with an extensive family education program holds a Friday night family Shabbat program. The program seems to be successful from the point of view of the participants but the case writer struggles with balancing his own educational goals with the social needs of participants.
- *Help the group determine what facts will be most useful in really understanding this case. It may be helpful to list them on the board.*

II. "WHAT IS THIS A CASE OF?"

In the groups with which we have studied this case, participants raised issues such as:
- Balancing educational and social goals (unclear goals)
- Institutional change
- Getting buy-in and sharing vision
- Evaluating success
- Inadequate curriculum
- Gap between leader's perceptions and those of the participants
- The problem of teaching Shabbat in the context of family education
- "Take Home"—what do families come away with?
- Must every event be meaningful to every participant?
- The vulnerability of the professional—accepting roles and maintaining integrity

Your group may come up with different or additional issues.

III. CASE ANALYSIS
- *At this point the discussion can go in any number of directions. You may want to begin by asking the group to choose one (or more) of the issues raised above as a focus by asking them which of the issues is most relevant to their practice. Or, as a facilitator, you may want to direct the conversation by choosing one (or more) of the issues raised and directing the discussion to meet your particular agenda for the group.*
- *For each of your discussion foci look at how that particular situation developed.*

How do the players themselves (the writer, the families) contribute to the situation?

What do we know about these programs?

What do we know about the educator? What is his attitude toward the program and the participants?

Is this a new problem? How is its "newness" (or not) related to the problem?

- *What did the family educator do, with what results, risks and consequences?*

- *How do you think the situation appeared to other participants and why do you think so?*

IV. INCORPORATING THE TEXT STUDY

- *How does our text study shed light on the case? (See "Large Group Discussion Point" #1.)*

- *Are there (other) Jewish value concepts that can help us see this issue from a Jewish perspective? See the list of "Big Jewish Ideas" in the appendix. For example: kavvana, ruach Shabbat–how do they apply to our situation?*

V. CASE EVALUATION

- *In your experience, is this situation typical?*

- *What might be other ways of handling this situation? What are the risks and benefits of each?*

- *After our discussion would you refine your idea about what this is a case of?*

- *What lingering questions do you have?*

VI. CLOSURE–REFLECTION ON PRACTICE

Journaling and/or reflection in small groups is optional.

- *Choose a question that invites participants to connect the issues raised in the case discussion to their own practice of family education.*

  For example: Have you ever felt challenged trying to balance your own educational goals with the social needs of your group? When? How have you handled it?

- *Ask participants to extrapolate principles of practice–generalizations of good practice that could guide them in their own work.*

- *And/or have participants write about an issue from the case that was not discussed.*

- *And/or have participants reflect on the case study process: What new insights did you gain from our discussion? What part of the discussion did you find most challenging?*

CASE #9
THE INDIAN
FOLK TALE

Text: Tochecha

TEXTS: 1) Leviticus 19:17 (Hebrew & English translation)

2) Babylonian Talmud, tractate Arachin 16b (Aramaic & English translation)

3) Babylonian Talmud, tractate Yevamot 65b (Aramaic & English translation)

4) Midrash Devraim Rabba 1:4 (Hebrew & English translation)

CONTEXT: Central to the ethical framework of traditional Judaism, *tochecha*—literally "rebuke"—is the imperative to offer criticism in order to restrain or rehabilitate a person or correct his or her behavior. The text from Leviticus is the Biblical mitzvah, and the other texts serve to limit its application.

Note: In text #4 Bilaam was an Aramean soothsayer who was asked by Balak, King of Moab, to curse the people of Israel who were encamped near them (Numbers 22). However, to Balak's surprise, Bilaam opened his mouth and a blessing came out instead.

QUESTIONS FOR STUDY IN HEVRUTA

NOTE: We divided the group into two and had half the group study the texts that were about giving *tochecha* (texts 1,2& 3) and half the group study the texts about receiving *tochecha* (texts 1 & 4).

1) According to text #1, what is the purpose of rebuking? What is the dangerous or difficult aspect of observing this mitzvah?

2) How does text #2 limit the giver of *tochecha*? What do you risk with "endless" rebuking?

3) How do the rabbis understand the verse from Proverbs (text #3) as further limiting the giver of *tochecha?* How would you know when someone really wants rebuke?

4) According to text #4, what kind of relationship between the two parties must exist in order for one to accept *tochecha* from another? What psychological insight does this piece of advice contain?

LARGE GROUP DISCUSSION POINTS—for the facilitator

1) Unpopularity. The mitzvah of *tochecha* is not an easy one. Think of a time when you were either the giver or recipient of *tochecha* in a teaching setting. Share your experience with the group (or a partner).

2) Teaching. Do you ever teach "unpopular" mitzvot to the families you work with? Give some examples. How can you imagine sharing this particular value with families? In what context?

Text Study
TEXT STUDY: GIVING TOCHECHA

I. Leviticus 19:17

You must not hate your brother in your heart, you must "*hoche-ach tochee-ach*" your neighbor, and not bear sin because of him.

לֹא־תִשְׂנָ֤א אֶת־אָחִ֙יךָ֙ בִּלְבָבֶ֔ךָ הוֹכֵ֤חַ תּוֹכִ֙יחַ֙ אֶת־עֲמִיתֶ֔ךָ וְלֹא־תִשָּׂ֥א עָלָ֖יו חֵֽטְא׃

II. Talmud Bavli, Arachin 16b

How far should rebuking go? Rav said: Until [the rebuker is] beaten up. Shmuel said: Until [the rebuker is] cursed. Rabbi Yochanan said: Until [the rebuker is] rebuked in return…

עד היכן תוכחה? רב אומר: עד הכאה ושמואל אמר: עד קללה ורבי יוחנן אמר: עד נזיפה.

III. Talmud Bavli, Yevamot 65b

Rabbi El'a stated in the name of Rabbi Elazar son of Rabbi Shimon: As one is commanded to say that which will be listened to, so is one commanded not to say that which will not be listened to. Abba stated: It is [this is one's] obligation as it says, "Don't rebuke a scoffer, for they will hate you; rebuke a sage and they will love you." (Proverbs 9:8)

ואמר רבי אילעא משום ר' אלעזר בר' שמעון: כשם שמצוה על אדם לומר דבר הנשמע כך מצוה על אדם שלא לומר דבר שאינו נשמע. רבי אבא אומר: חובה שנאמר: (משלי ט') אל תוכח לץ פן ישנאך הוכח לחכם ויאהבך.

TEXT STUDY: RECEIVING TOCHECHA

I. Leviticus 19:17

You must not hate your brother in your heart, you must *"hoche-ach tochee-ach"* your neighbor, and not bear sin because of him.

לֹא־תִשְׂנָ֥א אֶת־אָחִ֖יךָ בִּלְבָבֶ֑ךָ הוֹכֵ֤חַ תּוֹכִ֙יחַ֙ אֶת־עֲמִיתֶ֔ךָ
וְלֹא־תִשָּׂ֥א עָלָ֖יו חֵֽטְא׃

II. Devarim Rabba 1:4

Rabbi Acha son of Rabbi Chanina: It should have been that the rebukes should have come from the mouth of Bilaam and the blessings from the mouth of Moshe. But if Bilaam had rebuked Israel, they would have said, Our enemy is rebuking us! If Moshe had blessed Israel, then the nations of the world would have said, Israel's lover is blessing them! So God said: Moshe who loves them should rebuke them and Bilaam who hates them should bless them. This way the blessings are rebukes would be assured.

א״ר אחא ב״ר חנינא ראויות היו התוכחות לומר
מפי בלעמוהברכות מפי משה אלא אילו הוכיחם
בלעם היו ישראל אומרים שונא מוכיחנו
ואילו ברכם משה היו אומות העולם אומרים אוהבן ברכן
אמר הקב״ה יוכיחן משה שאוהבן ויברכן בלעם
ששונאן כדי שיתבררו הברכות והתוכחות ביד ישראל.

Case #9: "The Indian Folk Tale"

"I don't understand what we are doing here and why I bothered to fight with my son over coming in order to waste our time with this type of discussion." Helen's comment came out of the blue at the end of what I had considered to be a successful family program.

We had begun the program, as usual, by creating a living room within the space of the small sanctuary in our small Orthodox synagogue. All the families gathered in a circle; parents in chairs and pillows on the floor, kids on laps or sitting on the rug. Mark, one of the fathers in our group and the husband of one of the planners, introduced the evening's topic—gratitude—with a folk tale from India. As he told the story, his three-year-old son Ben assisted by pulling various objects out of a paper bag to illustrate the story. Ben always had trouble sitting during our circle time introductions, and Mark had planned this drama with Ben at home to keep his attention focused. It made the story more engaging. After the story Mark asked the group certain pointed questions that led to our Jewish text about gratitude—the crossing of the Red Sea from Exodus 15.

Texts and study questions were distributed, and each family moved to find a comfortable space for *chevruta*-style study. Our program, called Family Chevruta, was the first attempt at family education in our synagogue. My colleague Hannah and I had spent hours writing the curriculum and sharing our ideas with a small committee that included the rabbi and two other volunteers. The group of ten families with children ranging in age from four to eleven years old had been meeting for several months. Many families in our community felt that standard family education wasn't for them. They felt that they were leading rich Jewish lives. They already knew how to keep *shabbat*, how to build a *Sukkah* and what was in a *mezuzah*.

Hannah and I came up with the idea of a program to encourage families to study text together, in which we would address a different topic and study a text from the Bible or *Mishna* each month. Our curriculum was based on the model of Vicky Kelman's *Family Room*,[1] in which a group of families met together once a month. Hannah and I, both teachers and family educators, did this project as volunteers for our own synagogue, and both our families were participating in the program.

This evening's program had developed in a way that was slightly different from the usual. Our original topic was anger—how do we, as Jews, look at anger? What do our rabbis tell us about anger and how to deal with it? We had chosen a text and had already prepared most of the activities when several parents called us, concerned that the topic was too negative. One parent, trying to be responsive to the needs of the community, suggested the topic of gratitude instead of anger, and we changed topics

---

[1] Vicky Kelman, *Family Room: Linking Families into a Jewish Learning Community*, The Shirley and Arthur Whizin Institute for Jewish Family Life of the University of Judaism (Los Angeles), 1995.

midstream. Hannah remembered a wonderful Indian folk tale, "A Drum," which she thought would be a great introduction to the new topic, and which she had used when teaching the idea of giving thanks in an Orthodox day school. As our text for study we chose Exodus 15, "The Song of the Sea," sung by Moshe and Miriam, which seemed to fit the topic perfectly. After several more hours of thought and preparation we were ready for our Sunday evening Family Hevruta. We had no idea what awaited us.

As families finished up their discussions and text study they gathered again in a circle to share their conclusions. There was lively discussion involving parents and kids. Most families had talked about being grateful for miracles, such as the crossing of the Red Sea, as well as the more difficult issue of saying thank you for everyday miracles. The concept of retribution (the Israelites' rejoicing that God had punished their enemies), which also arose in this Biblical passage, did not come up in the group discussion.

After the group discussion we broke for dinner. The kids ate quickly and went outside to play, and the parents gathered together to discuss our next meeting. Out of the blue–or so it seemed to me–Helen, one of the most educated parents, spoke out emotionally. "I think that we are sugarcoating the Torah for our children. This is not a text about gratitude. It is a text about retribution. There are certain realities in life. Bad things do happen to the Jewish people. Is it so terrible to want retribution? What do we want to teach our children? Sometimes I am thankful when bad things happen to those who hate us and hurt us as a people, and I think my child can deal with this."

There was silence among the other parents. Then Mark commented, "But Helen, we were talking about gratitude and trying to use this text to show how the Israelites were grateful to *HaShem* (God) for His miracles." Helen shot back angrily, "If you wanted to discuss gratitude, you should have chosen a different text. I can think of ten better examples than this one. And why did we begin the discussion with a story from another culture? Our tradition is rich in stories to share with our children. An Indian folk tale adds nothing to their perspective about their own culture."

I remained quiet during this entire interchange. I wanted to say, "If you know so much, why haven't you been helping us with the planning? We are volunteering our precious free time and would have welcomed your input. This is not a closed committee." But I didn't say what I really thought. My main concern was to somehow reframe the discussion in a more positive way. Helen had a very strong influence on the group. Her remarks had changed a relaxed, positive atmosphere to one of negative hostility. The children were returning, and it was time to say *Birkat HaMazon*. Mark and I suggested that we choose a time to continue this discussion. Several parents volunteered to follow up on our suggestion. After *Birkat HaMazon* we dispersed, with no resolution or closure. Helen's questions and objections still hung in the air. The evening had changed from a cheerful positive study session to a question mark as to where to go from here.

As a result of this incident, both Hannah and I resigned from the planning committee. I approached the board of the synagogue to hire a paid teacher to work on planning and to lead the group until the end of the year; they agreed. Hannah and I continued to participate with our families as did Helen and her family. We never discussed what happened that night, and it remained a shadow over the program for the rest of the year.

Thinking again about this incident, the following questions remain:

- Should we have set some guidelines from the beginning as to how to handle conflict, especially in light of the fact that the leaders and planners were volunteers in the same community as the rest of the group?
- Why didn't someone call Helen to resolve the conflict?
- How can volunteers within a community remain professional although they are working with friends and fellow congregants?

Commentary by Judy Israel Elkin

You know the oft-quoted saying: "Everyone should have two pockets to hold two notes"–in one pocket, a note that reads "I am but dust and ashes," and in the other a note reading "The world was created for my sake." We should take things we do seriously, but not too seriously, for we can only control and be held responsible for so much. What am I getting at? Helen was poised for a fight the minute she walked into that synagogue–actually well before she arrived at the *shul*, when she was fighting with her son to join her for this program. And, as we know, there are many Helens out there. (Sometimes, even we are Helens.) My commentary focuses not on Helen or on controlling Helen or even on co-opting Helen, but rather on the struggle of family educators, avocational and professional, to maintain our own integrity and the integrity of the endeavor.

If we anticipate that the Helens of the world will be in our programs, we will be derailed by them far less often. Family education is risky business. If we think it's hard to facilitate such programs, we should remind ourselves how hard it is to "be facilitated." Having one's parenting skills, relationships, ambivalences and Jewish commitments on display can be excruciating for many. Though I do not believe that one needs to be a social worker or psychologist to be a good family educator, I do believe that one has to be sensitive to these issues and hone that sensitivity as much as possible. Anticipating the baggage that people bring to us, without putting it in the pocket that confirms that we're but dust and ashes, is one of our many challenges.

People come to family education for many different reasons. We're not always sure what their motivations are, and many times *they* are not sure either. Sometimes people come to us for one reason but stay involved for another. We mustn't be fooled by the seemingly homogeneous nature of the group in this case. Though they *daven* in the same *shul* and perhaps even send their children to the same day school, they each come with their own unique story. They each traveled different roads to get to this point, bringing with them different ways of interpreting their individual experiences and the Jewish communal experience as well. Knowing this is critical as we hear and really listen to the people in our groups.

The sad ending of the case actually took me by surprise. I expected to hear about the results of the follow-up meeting with Mark and the narrator after the outburst. I expected to hear how Helen had influenced the content of the next session. We family educators must not only anticipate such outbreaks but be prepared to do our work despite them. If the project and the curriculum have integrity and if we are committed to the endeavor, we need to convey that with confidence. Clearly there is much we'll never know about this case. We can assume, however, that many complex details determined the outcome. Our job is to become comfortable with complex systems such as families and group dynamics and to understand that there are not only two sides to every story, but often three or four!

It is worth noting that after Helen's outburst the other parents were silent. Though there are many ways to interpret the silence, certainly one reading is that they didn't agree with her. Parents did not join in to concur with Helen's objections. My concern at that point would be for the rest of the parents. Their experience needs to be protected. This is not the time to debate with Helen, especially since there is too much emotional baggage attached to the discussion. I would have firmly said something like: "You know, Helen, you're bringing up some very important philosophical issues about Jewish education and education in general. It's an important conversation to have, but for a lot of reasons this doesn't seem to be the right time and place. Can we get together some time next week with the committee and the rabbi to consider your philosophical stance? I'll give you a call tomorrow to set up a time. Thanks for raising it." This would validate her ideas while checking her affect and process. Reestablishing boundaries is one of the things we have to monitor from time to time.

In this case no one follows through on their intention to meet with Helen to continue the conversation, and the issues she raised about content are not revisited in a deeper way. This strikes a chord, because I worry that following up on our programs is less common than creating inspiring programs. Follow-up programs are harder than first programs. They require more depth of thought, new goals, individualized considerations, and new marketing gimmicks. I'm concerned in general about the ability to keep people involved past the neophyte stage. We've become quite adept at getting people through our doors and into our *shuls*, classrooms, JCCs and homes. How do we keep them coming? Should we? When is the appropriate time for weaning to begin? Is there such a thing as a family who doesn't "need" family education? What would that family look like, and what kind of support does it continue to need?

This case has a lot to teach about volunteerism and the avocational teacher. Much has been written in the field of Jewish education (see, for example, the work of Sharon Feiman Nemser[1]) about the avocational teacher in Jewish congregational schools. How such teachers are trained and supported will determine their success and longevity in Jewish education. Though the rabbi meets with the lay team to review the curriculum, it does not seem that in this case they received real professional development either in Judaica or in education. Further, nothing is said about the mentoring that either Hannah or the author received. Lastly, we don't hear the words of the rabbi or president urging them to stay on or offering help and support. Why?

With the teacher shortage crippling every stream of Jewish education, recruiting talented and committed lay people to teach in our schools is an obvious solution. More than that, it is a brilliant way of modeling within the community the kinds of values and attitudes we hope to teach. We cannot however, embark on such a path without

---

[1] "Teach Them Diligently To Your Children: An Experience in Avocational Teaching", Sharon Feiman Nemser (Religious Education, 1997, issue #4) and "Beyond Prepared Material: Fostering Teacher Learninig in the Service of Children's Learning", Sharon Feiman Nemser and Gail Zaiman Dorph (Religious Education, 1997, issue #4).

the appropriate support structure in place. Empowering and training the avocational teacher (as well as the professional) is a responsibility of the field writ large.

But whether or not we involve lay people in the actual teaching of family education, we must at least pay attention to the synergy created when lay and professional work together sharing a vision and a common language. As professional family educators, we need to work hard to develop a strong and committed lay community that will not only support our work, but also take part in it.

Lastly, this case asks us to consider the questions of what are appropriate goals in Jewish family education and how we can achieve them. To review—The original topic for the session was anger, which was changed to gratitude because of input received from outside the planning group. Ironically, Helen's outburst and subsequent complaints suggest that the original topic might have been worth pursuing after all. The questions we are left with are: How are goals determined? Who should be involved in setting goals? What are appropriate goals for Jewish family education? and Are controversial subjects to be avoided, or can they constructively contribute to the overall goal(s)? Initially there was an interest in, in fact a preference for, addressing a difficult, even controversial topic, which was then abandoned. When the Helen's outburst raised a different difficult topic, it was also seemingly rejected.

Certainly Helen's delivery of her message had a lot to do with its reception. But let us consider the merits of the topics of anger and divine retribution. Within this milieu, a very appropriate goal might be to struggle with difficult texts—a goal, either topic would fit nicely. Every milieu is, of course, unique. In this community, involving more of the participants in setting goals would have enabled the facilitators to defend their choices of texts and discussion topics more confidently. In some cases, family educators set the goals for their constituencies, and in other settings they do so together with participants.

Whether goals are set by lay/professional committees, by the whole community, or by the professionals alone, it is clear that the articulated goals must dictate the program and not vice versa. Agreed-upon and clearly articulated goals guide our practice, inform our decisions and allow us to evaluate our work. Reaching consensus about goals can be very time-consuming and frustrating, taking many meetings and much compromise. If we don't bother, however, we run the risk of time-consuming and frustrating meetings *later* in the process (when as here, participants may vent their pent-up dissatisfactions). And even with agreed-upon goals, Helen might still have "flipped out."

Lastly we should learn something about reflective practice from this case. This case was written for the sake of teaching family educators and contributing to the field of family education. I think the process of writing down some of our own challenging cases would be incredibly helpful to all of us. Carving out the time to write about what we do is almost impossible, but no more impossible than many of the other things we do for the families we teach. The insights we will gain about family education in general and our own practice in particular will be worthwhile. Perhaps it was as the result of a similar process that the teacher long ago, who wrote about the challenge of being a human being, taught us about what we should have in our two pockets. Thanks to that teacher the task is a made a little easier for us.

Commentary by Amy Grossblatt Pessah

"The Indian Folk Tale" raises two major questions:

1. How can one be both a volunteer and participant simultaneously? and
2. How do we, as family educators, respond to parents who act inappropriately?

The challenges of volunteering. Many parents in our synagogues and schools volunteer in various capacities and in varying degrees. In our case study two teachers who were family educators and participants in their synagogue's Family Hevruta program volunteered to plan the curriculum. They were members of the small Family Hevruta planning committee along with the rabbi and two other volunteers. Given their numerous hours spent planning and considering what texts to use and how to maximize the other participants' experience, it is no wonder that they felt very frustrated when one participant publicly critiqued the content of the program.

While reading this case study, I wondered whether the other families in the Family Hevruta program knew that the planning committee existed. Did the families know how much planning time and energy was volunteered by the family educators? Did the families receive guidelines prior to participating in such a program? If these matters had been addressed at an introductory meeting with the participants, as discussed below, future problems might have been avoided. At an initial meeting with the families, after welcoming them to the program, the educators or leaders could introduce those involved in the planning and advise them of the amount of time devoted to the process and. more important, the goals of the programs and the methods of achieving them. In our case, if the families had been told from the outset that there may be times when stories or texts from non-Jewish cultures are used, perhaps Helen's objection to the Indian tale might been avoided. Or perhaps Helen would have voiced her discomfort with non-Jewish sources at this introductory meeting and the group could have decided at that time which texts to use throughout the program.

In addition to explaining the overall framework for the entire program at the introductory session, the leader should also outline guidelines at each individual session. Families need to know as they study each text that, even though there may be several lessons that to learn from that text, the discussion should focus on the designated topic.[1]

Topics for the year should also be discussed at the introductory session. Perhaps the families could rank their top several choices on a list of possible topics. Empowering

---

[1] While we family educators may desire the conversation to remain on target, we should not to remain be so focused on our own agenda that we miss out on an unplanned learning opportunity.

families to choose what they want to study will not only help to prevent complaints, but also provide them with a sense of partnership in the program's evolution.

On the specific subject of criticizing the program, the facilitators should discuss how to offer criticism constructively. While we presume that more family input will mean less criticism of the program, sometimes criticism cannot be avoided. Families should be encouraged to offer constructive criticism tactfully and privately. The educator can also emphasize Judaism's ability to relate to all areas of life, including how we respond to others and how to best offer criticism. They might create a mini-lesson, in the Family Hevruta model, using the text "We learn in the Talmud that embarrassing someone in public is like committing murder."[2] A discussion or project might then develop around this issue. By having the families talk about this text, not only will they become familiarized with the method of Hevruta study to be used throughout the year, but the text itself will become more meaningful and will help ensure that any public criticism during the program will be constructive.

Responding to parental criticism. Even if guidelines or ground rules are presented at the beginning of a program, there will be times when participants behave or respond inappropriately.[3] Family educators and facilitators must learn how to handle these tense and awkward situations. By observing the clues sent by the participants that indicate discontent or dissatisfaction (such as body language, facial expressions, or vocal remarks), we will be able to monitor their reactions to the program. In our case study, did Helen send any earlier signals that she was unhappy with the Indian folk tale? How had she reacted during previous programs?

Family educators also must be attuned to the affective, as well as the cognitive, part of their programming, in order to be prepared to respond appropriately to inappropriate comments; for example, they will know whether blow-ups come out of the blue or from a chronically discontented participant.

If the educator notices a pattern of dissatisfaction on the part of a chronically discontented participant, she might preempt the blow-up by speaking to that participant privately between programs and trying to understand what s/he finds problematic. If you find the comments helpful, the facilitator might suggest that the participant become involved in assisting to make changes in future programs.

Comments that come as a surprise will catch us off guard and will probably put us on the defensive; nonetheless, we must respond. I used to find myself tongue-tied when placed in an uncomfortable situation and therefore conceived a "standard response" which I kept ready to use as needed: "I would like to understand better exactly what you mean, but now is not the best time to talk about it. However, I will give you a call

---

[2]Babylonian Talmud, Bava Metzia 58b, "A *tanna* taught the following *b'reita* before Rav Nachman bar Yitzchak, 'Anyone who shames another person in public is as if he sheds his blood [because his face gets white, implying that the blood has been taken out].' "

[3]By "inappropriate" I mean comments that are counterproductive to the goals of the program and to building group cohesion. While parents should be encouraged to share their differing opinions and perspectives with the group, counterproductive comments should be nipped in the bud. The family educator must use her judgment to determine whether the comments shared will further the goals of the overall program or detract from them.

tomorrow so we can discuss things in more detail." With this response, I have been able to react immediately and follow up with the individual at a more appropriate time.

In the case study, Helen's comment at the end of the evening was certainly inappropriate, but the fact that it was never addressed is even more troubling. We must address such comments in a timely manner, to indicate explicitly to the participants that we are in charge of the program and able to be flexible and amenable to change. We also implicitly serve as a role model by exhibiting a Jewish way of responding that protects the integrity and dignity of all involved.

Resolving the conflict. In our case study, we do not know whether Helen's comment should or could have been anticipated, but we do know that two problems arose from her remarks: hurt feelings between Helen and the group leaders and impact on the group—specifically, the rocky ending of the Family Hevruta session. Unfortunately, the family educators never resolved Helen's comment, and it "remained a shadow over the program for the rest of the year." We can understand how awkward it would have been for family educators to speak with Helen inasmuch as they were fellow participants in the group and fellow congregants. Nevertheless, follow-up was required, if not by the facilitators, then perhaps by the rabbi as mediator with Helen, the two leaders and Mark.

How could the leaders have retrieved the evening for the rest of the group? A concluding comment could have helped to diffuse the negative energy that permeated the group and to end the evening on a more positive note, even if it did not mitigate Helen's outburst. Perhaps the leaders could have wrapped up the evening by recentering the discussion on the text studied that evening. They could have concluded with something along the lines of "It is obvious that we have a discrepancy of opinion here, but let's focus on what we discussed in our program this evening. We read in Exodus 15:13, 'In Your love You lead the people You redeemed; In Your strength You guide them to Your holy abode.' Despite our differences, we are all part of *B'nei Yisrael*." By concluding with such a remark the leaders would have reminded the families of their ultimate reason for participating—studying holy texts with their family, as part of a larger community.

Concluding thoughts. Making these comments is obviously easier after reading this case study several times. The challenge comes when we, as family educators, must react immediately or when we are caught off guard. Although there are no simple equations, as family and human dynamics have too many complex components, the more experience we have in responding, the easier it will become. It is also important to realize that inappropriate remarks are often not directed at us or at the programs themselves, but are manifestations of other issues with which the participants are struggling. Although we should not take every remark personally, we must be open to criticism and change when it is needed and appropriate.

By planning ahead and thinking through each program, by anticipating any challenges that we may encounter, and by monitoring the reactions of our families, we can try to avoid potential conflicts. Preparation does not guarantee smooth sailing, but it certainly helps to set our course, with the hope of minimizing potential problems and maximizing the success of our programs.

Annotated Lesson Plan
(Notes for the Facilitator)

I. CASE OVERVIEW

- *Facilitator's Summary:* A small Orthodox synagogue begins their foray into family education with a monthly program that brings ten families together for text study. At one meeting the educator (a volunteer and member of the group) is challenged by Helen, a Jewishly knowledgeable parent with a strong influence on the group. Helen's challenge paralyzes the case writer and creates tension at the gathering. Following the incident the case writer resigns. The writer is left with lingering questions about group process, group facilitation and her own role in the incident.

- *Help the group determine what facts will be most useful in really understanding this case. It may be helpful to list them on the board.*

II. "WHAT IS THIS A CASE OF?"

In the groups with which we have studied this case, participants raised issues such as:

- A challenging participant
- Being a volunteer in your own community
- Diversity within a group
- Vulnerability of the professional
- Surprise
- Managing group facilitation and group dynamics
- Defining family education—Is it just for beginners?
- Goal setting
- The challenges of planning

Your group may come up with different or additional issues.

III. CASE ANALYSIS

- *At this point the discussion can go in any number of directions. You may want to begin by asking the group to choose one (or more) of the issues raised above as a focus by asking them which of the issues is most relevant to their practice. Or, as a facilitator, you may want to direct the conversation by choosing one (or more) of the issues raised and directing the discussion to meet your particular agenda for the group.*

- *For each of your discussion foci look at how that particular situation developed.*
  How do the players themselves (Helen, Mark, the writer) contribute to the situation?

What do we know about this group and this program?

What do we know about the educator? What is her attitude toward the program? What is her attitude toward Helen and the other participants?

Why was Helen never confronted?

- *How do you think the situation appeared to other participants and why do you think so? Why were they silent?*

- *What did the family educator do, with what results, risks and consequences? Why did this cause the end of her role as facilitator?*

VI. INCORPORATING THE TEXT STUDY

- *How does our text study shed light on the case? (See "Large Group Discussion Point" #1.)*

- *Are there (other) Jewish value concepts that can help us see this issue from a Jewish perspective? See the list of "Big Jewish Ideas" in the appendix. For example: kavod, derech eretz, talmud Torah, mehila, tochecha—how do they apply to our situation?*

V. CASE EVALUATION

- *In your experience, is this situation typical?*

- *What might be other ways of handling this situation? What are the risks and benefits of each?*

- *After our discussion would you refine your idea about what this is a case of?*

- *What lingering questions do you have?*

VI. CLOSURE—REFLECTION ON PRACTICE

Journaling and/or reflection in small groups is optional.

- *Choose a question that invites participants to connect the issues raised in the case discussion to their own practice of family education.*

  For example: What can you do in an explosive situation? What advice might you have given the case writer regarding "damage control" afterwards?

- *Ask participants to extrapolate principles of practice—generalizations of good practice that could guide them in their own work.*

- *And/or have participants write about an issue from the case that was not discussed.*

- *And/or have participants reflect on the case study process: What new insights did you gain from our discussion? What part of the discussion did you find most challenging?*

CASE #10
KAREN & SALLY

Text: Kaddish DeRabanan

TEXT: *Kaddish DeRabanan* (traditional text in Aramaic & English and Debbie Friedman's version)

CONTEXT: *Kaddish* means sanctification in Aramaic (the *lingua franca* of the Jewish community in which this prayer was composed). There are five different types of *kaddish* (including the mourner's *kaddish*). The original *kaddish* is the *kaddish deRabanan*—the rabbinical *kaddish*—originally recited by teachers and preachers at the end of a lesson as a formal way to dismiss their students.

QUESTIONS FOR STUDY IN HEVRUTA

1) What is the significance of a piece of liturgy that honors teachers, students and Torah study?

2) Look at the paragraph that mentions teachers and students. How does that part fit into the rest of *kaddish*?

3) Compare Debbie Friedman's version with the special paragraph in the original *kaddish*. What has she added? What has she omitted? In what context can you imagine using either her song or the original version?

LARGE GROUP DISCUSSION POINT—for the facilitator

Teachers of Teachers: What do the words of the *kaddish deRabanan* imply about family education? The boundaries between student and teacher may be fluid (in certain contexts a parent might teach a child or vice versa). There are also many different ways of teaching and being Torah. If we think of ourselves as both teacher and student when we facilitate family education experiences, we may become more comfortable in our role.

Text Study

Kaddish De Rabanan—Whom Have We Taught

May God's name be exalted and sanctified in the world which has been created according to God's own will and may God rule God's kingdom in your lifetime and in your days, and in the lifetime of the entire house of Israel, speedily in the near future—and say Amen.

May God's great Name be blessed forever and for all eternity. Blessed and praised, glorified, and exalted and uplifted, honored and elevated and extolled be the Name of the Holy One, blessed is God; above all the blessings and hymns, praises and consolations which we utter in the world—and say Amen.

May there be upon Israel, and upon our Sages, and upon their students, and upon all the students of their students, and upon all those who engage in Torah study in this land and in every land (for them and for us all), abundant peace, favor and kindness, compassion, long life, ample sustenance and redemption from the Father who is in heaven and on earth—and say Amen.

May there be abundant peace from heaven and a good life for all Israel, and say—Amen. May God who makes peace in the high heavens, in mercy, make peace for us and for all Israel—and say Amen.

יִתְגַּדַּל וְיִתְקַדַּשׁ שְׁמֵהּ רַבָּא.
בְּעָלְמָא דִּי בְרָא כִרְעוּתֵיהּ,
וְיַמְלִיךְ מַלְכוּתֵיהּ בְּחַיֵּיכוֹן וּבְיוֹמֵיכוֹן
וּבְחַיֵּי דְכָל בֵּית יִשְׂרָאֵל.
בַּעֲגָלָא וּבִזְמַן קָרִיב וְאִמְרוּ אָמֵן:

יְהֵא שְׁמֵהּ רַבָּא מְבָרַךְ
לְעָלַם וּלְעָלְמֵי עָלְמַיָּא:

יִתְבָּרַךְ וְיִשְׁתַּבַּח וְיִתְפָּאַר וְיִתְרוֹמַם
וְיִתְנַשֵּׂא וְיִתְהַדָּר וְיִתְעַלֶּה וְיִתְהַלָּל
שְׁמֵהּ דְּקֻדְשָׁא בְּרִיךְ הוּא
לְעֵלָּא (בעשי״ת וּלְעֵלָּא מִכָּל)
מִן כָּל בִּרְכָתָא וְשִׁירָתָא
תֻּשְׁבְּחָתָא וְנֶחֱמָתָא,
דַּאֲמִירָן בְּעָלְמָא, וְאִמְרוּ אָמֵן:

עַל יִשְׂרָאֵל וְעַל רַבָּנָן,
וְעַל תַּלְמִידֵיהוֹן
וְעַל כָּל תַּלְמִידֵי תַלְמִידֵיהוֹן,
וְעַל כָּל מָאן דְּעָסְקִין בְּאוֹרַיְתָא,
דִּי בְאַתְרָא הָדֵין
וְדִי בְכָל אֲתַר וַאֲתַר.
יְהֵא לְהוֹן וּלְכוֹן
שְׁלָמָא רַבָּא, חִנָּא וְחִסְדָּא
וְרַחֲמִין, וְחַיִּין אֲרִיכִין,
וּמְזוֹנֵי רְוִיחֵי, וּפֻרְקָנָא,
מִן קֳדָם אֲבוּהוֹן
דִּי בִשְׁמַיָּא וְאַרְעָא וְאִמְרוּ אָמֵן.

יְהֵא שְׁלָמָא רַבָּא מִן שְׁמַיָּא,
וְחַיִּים וְטוֹבִים
עָלֵינוּ וְעַל כָּל יִשְׂרָאֵל וְאִמְרוּ אָמֵן.
עֹשֶׂה שָׁלוֹם בִּמְרוֹמָיו הוּא
יַעֲשֶׂה בְרַחֲמָיו שָׁלוֹם
עָלֵינוּ וְעַל כָּל יִשְׂרָאֵל, וְאִמְרוּ אָמֵן:

Kaddish De Rabanan

Debbie Friedman has written and composed this version of *Kadish D'Rabanan:*

For our teachers and their students
And the students of our students.
We ask for peace and loving kindness.
And let us say, Amen.

And for those who study Torah
Here and everywhere
May they be blessed with all they need
And let us say, Amen.

We ask for peace and loving kindness.
And let us say, Amen.

The Case

"Rabbi, you will be there for the beginning of the program, won't you?" asked my secretary as I was running between classrooms before the start of Sunday school.

"I'll be there when I get there," I said.

"But Karen and Sally are really worried. They want you there for the *whole* program."

"Tell them I want to greet families in the parking lot as they come in and check on a few things, and I will be there as soon as I can. They can start without me!"

"Okay, but they are real nervous."

I began to wonder. Karen and Sally are both very experienced teachers. Between them they have over forty years of teaching experience in supplementary schools. Neither of them is new to our congregation. Furthermore, we ran this exact same program last year, and it was successful. Why were they so nervous?

Sally has been the star Hebrew teacher in our school, which I direct, for over ten years and is a master teacher. The kids love her. She has the ability to really inspire kids. For the last several years she has also been teaching Hebrew as well as the Judaica unit for the fifth grade.

Karen has also taught the fifth grade for several years in our school and, before joining our faculty, had worked full-time in another congregation in a leadership role. She is a credentialed teacher who teaches in the local public schools as well. She is very well liked and has always seemed to be an effective and creative teacher.

During the past several years we have devoted several faculty meetings to planning family education programs for the school and have participated in "in-service" professional development in the field of family education.

Several years ago I approached Sally about expanding her skill set and invited her to a major family education training seminar. After a little bit of coaxing she joined me, the school committee chair and another of our rabbis at the conference. She really enjoyed the conference and came back inspired. After the conference I suggested to Karen and Sally that we consider making the fifth grade one of our intensive family education years. They asked what I had in mind. I told them about a published program I had seen for that age group, which I thought would be easy for them to adapt to their personalities and teaching styles. After having some time to study the curriculum I arranged a meeting for Sally, Karen and me with the author of the curriculum so that we could ask him how best to use his curriculum in our setting.

After three years of running and refining this family education program, Karen and Sally like its basic structure but are still *uncomfortable being in front of parents and try to avoid it at all costs.* For these three years I have always been the lead facilitator for the program. Although Karen and Sally have had the chance to observe me (I think

I was a good role model), they have not yet been able to take on the leadership role themselves.

This particular Sunday morning program, planned in consultation with the author of the curriculum, was to be the second of five special family programs for the fifth grade during the course of the year. It was a program that we knew worked well, for we had used it last year with very positive feedback.

Last month Karen and Sally had led the kick-off event for this program by themselves, because I had to be at another program at the same time. They were not happy about doing it, but both reported that the program had gone well. I had also heard good feedback from participants and knew that the program had gone well because most of the families showed up for the second program. (If last month's program had not gone well, there was no way that we would have had a good turnout for the second program.)

This morning I was a few minutes late getting to the social hall. Sally and Karen had everything set up but had not yet started the program. Families were milling about, getting coffee and greeting one another. I asked people to find seats and then, as per the lesson plan, I introduced Karen, who helped get the program started by leading a few songs. (Karen likes singing and has done it professionally, so I knew that she would be comfortable with this role.) After leading the singing, however, she became a wallflower for the rest of the morning.

Throughout the morning I served as the facilitator for the program, giving directions and leading large group discussions. Sally acted as a floater, checking to see how families were doing in their small discussions and helping to facilitate small groups.

At one point Sally turned to me and said, "It is really good when families see you leading this discussion. They respect it so much more when the rabbi is involved in these programs." I said, "I know that you can do it, too."

Our teachers all know that Family Education has been a major focus of the school and the congregation over the past several years. However, reflecting back on these two teachers, as well as the other good teachers who feel ambivalent about working with parents, the following questions come to mind:

- If these two very experienced teachers feel ambivalent and nervous at best about being in front of parents, how do my less experienced teachers feel?
- Have I allowed teachers to not learn a new skill set by doing it for them? Have I facilitated the teachers' ambivalence and discomfort by not forcing them to take more of a lead role in both the creation and implementation of our family education programs?
- Do we need to provide our teachers other forms of training so that they can become family educators?
- How can we help teachers see themselves as effective educators in a number of different roles? How can we help them expand their "repertoire"?
- Are we left with the dilemma that "you cannot teach an old dog new tricks"?

- Should we simply accept as a fact that not every teacher is cut out to be a family educator? What would that mean?
- How can we help our teachers to build self-confidence as they acquire a new skill set?
- How can we introduce family education into our school setting when the staff, though supportive, is reluctant or unwilling to lead?

Commentary by Jo Kay

I found it quite interesting to "sit in" on the conversation among the rabbi, Karen and Sally. It allowed me to "hear" and "see" some of the concerns and issues of clergy and educators regarding Family Education. Clearly, these issues will strike common chords with most of us trying to advance this field, while developing a level of comfort for all involved.

This case begins with an incident during the second of a series of five special family education programs for the fifth grade. We are told that although this program had been used successfully the previous year, and although the teachers had seen the rabbi run it and were completely familiar with it, they were still reluctant and apprehensive.

What is this a case of? Is it a case of two experienced teachers who are ambivalent about family education and uncomfortable working with parents or families? Is this a case of excellent teachers *of children* who are not excellent teachers *of adults*? Is it a case of inadequate training in working with families?

Suffice it to say, something else is going on here. Let's start from the beginning. Two excellent teachers have been identified by the principal/rabbi as possible family educators for a synagogue school. Unsure what family education actually is, what he may expect of them, and perhaps even why she is being asked, one of the teachers needs considerable convincing to join the rabbi at a major family education training seminar.

The first questions these teachers might ask themselves are: "Why do I need to attend a training seminar? Does the rabbi think I need to learn how to teach? Have my formerly successful teaching techniques paled or staled to the point that they are no longer valued? Am I losing it as a teacher? What's wrong with me and the way I work? Am I being asked to attend a "training seminar" because I need training? Are the families no longer happy with my teaching style? Is the school changing without my even realizing it?"

Taking certain steps earlier might have eased the apprehensions. Have there been discussions about family education with the whole faculty, from the *bima*, by the rabbis, at Parents' Association meetings and with the students? What has been done to educate the entire community about family education? What has been done to elicit ideas and cooperation? Articles and open forums might have increased the energy and excitement before the participants actually dove into the work.

Next, after the "training seminar," the rabbi suggested that the grade these *newly inspired teachers* teach become a grade of intensive family education. "What does this mean?" they must have asked, and a second stumbling block may have been erected. Instead of asking these skillful and creative teachers how *they* thought family education might be implemented in their grade, or how *they* would like to see the year develop, the rabbi handed them a pre-existing program he had identified and which he thought could be adapted. What might be happening here? Could the fears of these teachers regarding their own self-worth as successful practitioners have been shaken again? Might they again have questioned their own ability to come up with a successful program? Or might they have felt that they really didn't understand the rabbi's vision for the synagogue?

After being given the program to "study" they were to meet with its author to ask him how best to use his curriculum. In my experience, the best work (both in family education and in general education) comes from teachers who create their own programs from something they are truly excited about. Handing teachers a pre-existing program, and then asking the author how to use it, eliminates the possibility of personal creativity or, more significantly, the chance for the teachers to make it their own. The very reason these teachers were selected has been factored out of the equation. No wonder they struggle to take control of the program.

The teachers' discomfort in front of parents and their avoidance of it "at all costs" may also be directly related to their feeling of lack of ownership of the program; they didn't create it. It may not be in the subject areas in which they know they excelled and, more important, the rabbi has been the only role model they have seen lead the program. The stakes seem too high. The congregation and the school have had family education as a major focus for several years. Many faculty meetings and in-service professional development courses have been offered. Yet the teachers are reluctant—and not only these teachers.

Again we must ask, "What is happening here? Has the focus been on the teachers' need for training rather than on studying what family education is and can be in their own setting? Has the rabbi been the only role model? Is family education an *intrinsic* part of the school curriculum, or is it seen as external to and apart from the school curriculum—perhaps different from what the teachers are used to teaching?"

This is where it might be helpful to use the *Tzimtzum* model of education—that is, to step back and leave room for others to create. Let the teachers take the lead. Enable them to use their strengths, to draw on what is familiar to them (what they know and do well—in this case, Hebrew and music) and to experiment with this new material in a relaxed and supportive manner. If family education is to become the lens through which we frame all that is taught, we must be prepared to allow our teachers to frame it for their own work.

Other questions concern the rabbi's role. If the rabbi has always been the lead facilitator for three years, he has gone beyond serving as a role model for the teachers. This must be the "rabbi's thing." Parents, students and faculty have probably come to expect the rabbi to be around during each family education program and to be the person in charge. If so, how can the teachers take the lead? Has the school developed a family education culture or expectation tied to the clergy? Do the teachers feel that only the rabbi can be successful in this arena, and that success is really important to the rabbi? Do the teachers feel supported by the rabbis, or do they feel that they are supporting the rabbis? Where is the "team" in all this? How can the rabbis create a sense that they (rabbis, teachers, parents and students) are all in this together, and that if a program doesn't work, they will *all* return to the drawing boards? The pressure needs to be taken off these few programs, and the whole concept of family education needs to be normalized.

The school might consider having small, class-sized family education experiences several times a year in each class. The teachers might be asked to build these experiences around something they are already teaching. Perhaps each class's individual series of programs could include material for families to do at home and parent-only sessions, as well as family sessions. Parents might be polled to determine if the area of focus is of interest to them or whether the teacher might better organize the material to meet the parents' needs. Starting small may be less daunting. The teachers would be in charge of their own work, and the successes and failures would feel more manageable. Once teachers have had several successes of their own, they may be more open to working with other teachers and more comfortable leading and watching other teachers lead. They might be more open to planning and running larger and more involved programs (but programs *they* have created or have been involved in creating).

Finally, this is more a case of ownership than a case of ambivalence. Teachers who are talented, creative and inspiring are capable of creating the family education programs they will run. They have strengths and skills they can draw upon. The idea that family education is a framework for thinking about education is exciting in itself—that is what we must convey to our faculties and our congregations. Teachers must believe in the value and the importance of this work if they are to move forward as educators interested in and comfortable with the sacred task of educating whole families.

Commentary by Nina J. Mizrahi

The case of "Karen and Sally" calls into question the efficacy of a teacher-based paradigm of family education. It is clear that the teachers' reluctance is not related to their mastery of the material, but to the inherent tensions in the relationship between parents and religious school teachers. Through experience and experimentation with various models of family education, I have come to understand the dynamics causing these tensions and to realize that a healthier, more parent-child-centered family education paradigm can be facilitated more comfortably and productively by the teacher.

In many religious schools, when a conflict arises, teachers may use the rabbi or principal as a buffer between the parents and themselves, preventing the teacher, parent and child from learning to resolve their conflicts independently. Parents and teachers need to be encouraged to form trusting relationships based on the belief that both can work together to help the child become an educated and practicing Jew.

As is the case in any relationship, fear of failure can lead to defensiveness or to struggles over control. Teachers may assume that parents will be resistant, even hostile, to the process of Jewish education—that parents will neither support the teacher nor involve themselves in Jewish learning. These assumptions can have a powerfully negative impact on the educational process. In some cases, a less knowledgeable or less experienced teacher may also feel inadequate and fear that he or she may be "found out" as incompetent.

Conversely, parents—whose own Jewish education or experiences may have been lacking or unpleasant—may express negative or ambivalent feelings toward the synagogue generally, or toward the teacher specifically. They may feel embarrassed that, despite their success in the "real" world, they know little about Judaism, and they may feel infantilized and uncomfortable every time they walk into the building. They may be unclear about why they are providing their child with a Jewish education or what they expect their child to learn. Or, if intermarried, they may feel guilty or resentful toward the Jewish community, especially if the intermarriage continues to raise painful or irreconcilable issues in the marriage.

Some parents are simply stressed out by the daily demands they of their jobs, their marriages, child-rearing or dealing with aging, infirm family members. Short of time, they find it impossible to enjoy—much less engage more fully in—their child's Jewish education. Their insecurities and busy schedules may also keep them from participating in their own Jewish learning. Certainly, this is all enough to create feelings of resistance, defensiveness and seeing the teacher as making unreasonable demands. Thus teachers and parents are caught in a triangulated nightmare, with the child in the middle.

Keeping this in mind, we return to the religious school-based family education program. In a teacher-centered model, the parent and child both become students of the teacher, and the teacher faces the challenge of speaking to both target groups on their respective levels simultaneously. When the rabbi serves as facilitator, he may struggle less with this dynamic, because he generally relates to families as families more often, particularly during services and life cycle events. The religious school teachers, however, work in a more "segregated" system. While they may be totally comfortable with their students in the safety of their classrooms, they may feel uncomfortable exposing themselves to the parents. They may view the parent-teacher relationship as one that is in conflict over the child, instead of recognizing the inherent connection our tradition makes between *moreh* (teacher) and *horeh* (parent).

If the teacher focuses the lesson toward the children, the parents may not feel engaged and may become passive observers. By the same token, the teacher may lose the children when we target the parents, making the child the passive observer. Either way, the experience does not engage the parent and child together in a meaningful way. The parent remains dependent upon the teacher for information, rather than feeling transformed and empowered to navigate independently through this Jewish experience.

In a parent-child-centered model, in contrast, the teacher becomes an active observer. Parents are called upon to apply, in a Jewish setting, parenting skills they already possess. This family-centered model empowers the parents while freeing the teacher from the role as "official Jew" and surrogate parent. The teacher becomes a facilitator of the experience that takes place between parent and child. This facilitation begins prior to the formal program when the educator plans a program that is both manageable and challenging. It continues when setting the tone of the program and when helping parents and their children process their experiences at appropriate points during the program. Observing a parent-child-centered program, one hardly notices the teacher. Instead, one sees pairs or triads of parents and children involved in learning together. In these transformative *hevruta* moments, insecurities and hostilities can fall away and be replaced by the joy of sharing a special moment of learning together.

For this parent-child-centered model to work, an additional level of preparation is needed. The program should be designed to be as self-explanatory as possible. Background information that might be needed for participants to participate most fully should be included in an easily accessible way. Written directions must be clear and concise. The program should set the parents up to succeed by incorporating skills and strengths they are expected to have. Activities should maximize parent-child interaction and facilitate growth by both.

Even if teachers have not created the program, they should be asked for input, including their own insights as parents. Perhaps they can be more involved in planning and running the program. Their family education training should include insights into parenting issues associated with particular age groups. Teachers should also receive training in discussion facilitation to learn how to extract insights and ideas from participants in an inviting and non-judgmental way.

Addressing the case of reluctant family educators in our school, after meeting with teachers and parents separately, has led us to understand that more needs to be done to encourage positive interactions between parents and teachers. Currently the parents seem more open than the teachers, but slowly we are beginning to break down the barriers. As we begin implementing this parent-child-centered approach we are noticing that parents, children and teachers are responding to family education with greater openness, comfort and enthusiasm.

Annotated Lesson Plan
(Notes for the Facilitator)

I. CASE OVERVIEW

- *Facilitator's Summary:* In a religious school that is very committed to family education, two experienced teachers are reluctant to lead family education programs without the active involvement of the rabbi/school principal. They have had limited professional development in the field of family education. The case writer perceives their dependence as problematic and is puzzled about how to enable these teachers to take a more active role.

- *Help the group determine what facts will be most useful in really understanding this case. It may be helpful to list them on the board.*

II. "WHAT IS THIS A CASE OF?"

   In the groups with which we have studied this case, participants raised issues such as:

- Who can/should/wants to be a family educator?

- Teachers of children asked to become teachers of parents, too

- Getting buy-in and commitment

- Adapting a curriculum to meet the strengths of the teachers

- Lack of role definition

- A rabbi-centric system: rabbi giving legitimacy to a program from the perspective of the teachers and the participants

- Need for good communication, shared vision and clear expectations (from all parties)

- Inadequate professional development

   Your group may come up with different or additional issues.

III. CASE ANALYSIS

- *At this point the discussion can go in any number of directions. You may want to begin by asking the group to choose one (or more) of the issues raised above as a focus by asking them which of the issues is most relevant to their practice. Or, as a facilitator, you may want to direct the conversation by choosing one (or more) of the issues raised and directing the discussion to meet your particular agenda for the group.*

- *For each of your discussion foci look at how that particular situation developed.*

   What role did mutual misunderstanding play?

   How do the players themselves (Karen, Sally, the rabbi, the school secretary) contribute to the situation?

What do we know about the rabbi? What is his/her attitude toward family education?

What do we know about the history of this particular program?

How would you characterize the rabbi's attitude toward the Karen and Sally?

- *What did the rabbi do, with what results, risks and consequences?*
- *How do you think the situation appeared to participants and why do you think so?*

IV. INCORPORATING THE TEXT STUDY

- *How does our text study shed light on the case? (See "Large Group Discussion Point" #1.)*
- *Are there (other) Jewish value concepts that can help us see this issue from a Jewish perspective? See the list of "Big Jewish Ideas" in the appendix. For example: sh'lom bayit or kavod—how do they apply to our situation?*

V. CASE EVALUATION

- *In your experience, is this situation typical? How can you relate the issues discussed to your own experience working with staff?*
- *What recommendations would you make to someone planning to engage a staff of teachers in creating and leading family education programs?*
- *After our discussion would you refine your idea about what this is a case of?*
- *What lingering questions do you have?*

VI. CLOSURE—REFLECTION ON PRACTICE

Journaling and/or reflection in small groups is optional.

- *Choose a question that invites participants to connect the issues raised in the case discussion to their own practice of family education.*

    For example: Who defines your role as a family educator? How clear is communication at your site vis-à-vis role definition and professional expectations? How could it be improved?

- *Ask participants to extrapolate principles of practice—generalizations of good practice that could guide them in their own work.*
- *And/or have participants write about an issue from the case that was not discussed.*
- *And/or have participants reflect on the case study process: What new insights did you gain from our discussion? What part of the discussion did you find most challenging?*

Appendix A:
A List of "Big Jewish Ideas"

The term "Big Jewish Ideas" is used to describe significant "value concepts" within Judaism that are essentially untranslatable. Below is a selection of "Big Jewish Ideas" that may be useful in the study of these particular cases.

Anivoot	humility
Derech Eretz	literally, "the way of the land," the way people are expected to behave, especially ethical behavior
Kavvana	intention, motive
Klal Yisrael	the community of Israel, refers to the inclusion of <u>all</u> of the Jewish people
Kedusha	holiness, sanctity
Mehila	pardon, forgiveness, reconciliation
Ruach Shabbat	the spirit of Shabbat, refers to the creation of a certain atmosphere and mood that is in keeping with the sanctity of the day
Sh'lom Bayit	literally "peace at home," compromising for the sake of other family members
Talmud Torah	the study of Torah, also, *divrei Torah,* words of Torah
Tefilla	prayer
Teshuva	repentance, return to God/good
Tochecha	offering criticism, rebuke

For more information see:

Teaching Jewish Virtues by Susan Freeman, A.R.E. Publishing.

The Dictionary of Jewish Words by Joyce Eisenberg and Ellen Scolnic, Jewish Publication Society, 2001.

—Contributor Biographies—

Harlene Appelman is Director of the Alliance for Jewish Education at the Jewish Federation of Metropolitan Detroit. She is on the faculty of the Whizin Institute for Jewish Family Life.

Charlene G. Bornstein is a resource specialist (special education) and a teacher for Santa Rosa City Schools (California).

Ellen Brosbe was Resource Associate for the Jewish Family Education Project at the Bureau of Jewish Education of San Francisco, the Peninsula, Marin and Sonoma Counties for the last seven years. She has served as visiting faculty at the Whizin Institute for Jewish Family Life. She is currently teaching seventh grade in a congregational school and is a consultant to the Jewish Family Education Project.

Shellie Dickstein is the Director of Family Education and Outreach for SAJES (the Suffolk Association for Jewish Educational Services serving Suffolk County, New York). She has served as a guest faculty member of the Whizin Institute.

Cindy Dolgin is the Director of Curriculum Development for Melton/United Synagogue's "Project Etgar," a Doctoral Candidate at Teacher's College—Columbia Unversity and former director of Education and Family Life at the Huntington Jewish Center (New York).

Judy Israel Elkin is a Family Educator on the staff of the BJE in Boston.

Marvin Goodman is the rabbi at Peninsula Sinai Congregation, Foster City, California. He is on the Advisory Committee of the Jewish Family Education Project of the San Francisco Bureau of Jewish Education.

Marian Gribetz is the Curator at the Jewish Women's Archives.

Joel Lurie Grishaver is the Creative Chair of Torah Aura Productions; the author of more than 70 books including *40 Things You Can Do to Save the Jewish People*, and is a on the faculty of the Whizin Institute.

Risa Munitz Gruberger is Dean of the Fingerhut School of Education at the University of Judaism and the former director of the Whizin Institute.

Janet Harris is the Director of Early Childhood Education at the Bernard Osher Marin Jewish Community Center in San Rafael, California. She is also the former Director of Camp Ramah Family Camp, Ojai, California.

Joan S. Kaye is the Executive Director of the Bureau of Jewish Education of Orange County, California and on the faculty of the Whizin Institute for Jewish Family Life.

Jo Kay is the Director of the New York School of Education at Hebrew Union College-Jewish Institute of Religion and on the faculty of the Whizin Institute. She is also the creator of the PACE (Parent and Child Education) family education model and continues to work as a family educator.

Eric Keitel is the Director of Development at the Mid-Peninsula Jewish Community Day School in Palo Alto, California.

Vicky Kelman is Director of the Jewish Family Education Project, at the Bureau of Jewish Education of San Francisco, the Peninsula, Marin and Sonoma Counties, author of many books and a Whizin Institute faculty member.

Sherry E. Knazan is the Family Educator at Congregation Kol Shofar, Tiburon, California. She is also a Family Education Fellow.

Patti Kroll is Director of Education at the Family Education Center of Congregation Beth Shalom, in Kansas City, Missouri.

Lisa Langer, RJE served as the Program Coordinator at Congregation Beth Am in Los Altos Hills, California for six years where she created and developed a variety of ongoing and one time family education programs. She is currently Community consultant for the Jewish Family Education Project and the School Services department at the Bureau of Jewish Education of San Francisco, the Peninsula, Marin and Sonoma counties.

Nina Mizrahi, RJE is the Director of the Pritzker Center for Jewish Education of the Jewish Community Centers of Chicago. Rabbi Mizrahi was ordained by HUC-JIR (NY) and is a certified Jewish Family Educator. Most recently, she received her Reform Jewish Educator certification.

Ronald Muroff is the rabbi of Chisuk Emuna Congregation in Harrisburg, Pennsylvania.

Esther Netter is the Executive Director of the Zimmer Children's Museum of Jewish Community Centers of Greater Los Angeles (formerly My Jewish Discovery Place) and the co-founder of the arts education initiative youTHink. She is on the faculty of the Whizin Institute.

Amy Grossblatt Pessah formerly the Pearlstone Director of Jewish Family Education at the Center for Jewish Education in Baltimore, Maryland, is currently practicing Jewish family education at home with her two sons, Josef and Eitan.

Irene Resnikoff is the Family Education and Hebrew Coordinator at Congregation Rodef Sholom in San Rafael California. Irene is also a Family Education Fellow.

Jeff Schein is on the faculty of the Cleveland College of Jewish Studies.

Stuart Seltzer is a Rabbi and Director of Education at Congregation Chizuh Amuno in Baltimore.

Rachel E. Sisk, MSW and MA in Jewish Communal Service was Director of Family Education at the Central Agency for Jewish Education in Miami, Florida. She has a certificate of Advanced Graduate Study in Jewish Family Education, and has been a guest faculty member of the Whizin Institute.

Andy Straus is rabbi of Temple Emanuel of Tempe, Arizona. Prior to that he served as the Associate Rabbi and Educational Director of Peninsula Temple Sholom, Burlingame California.

Sally Weber, LCSW, is Director of Jewish Community Programs at Jewish Family Service of Los Angeles. She has served as a faculty member for the Whizin Institute and the Hebrew Union College (L.A.). She has published articles on the changing Jewish family.

Joan Wolchansky is Director of Jewish Family Education and coordinator of Our Jewish Home at the Central Agency for Jewish Education in St. Louis, Missouri.

Ronald Wolfson is Vice President and Director of the Whizin Center for the Jewish Future at the University of Judaism. He pioneered Jewish family trips to Israel, professional development for Jewish family educators, and is author of "The Art of Jewish Living" series.

Staff

Rachel Brodie was a consultant for the Jewish Family Education Project at the Bureau of Jewish Education of San Francisco, the Peninsula, Marin and Sonoma Counties from 1997-2001. She is a graduate of the Jewish Family Educator's Training Institute of the Board of Jewish Education (New York). She was the primary facilitator of the Common Ground seminar for four years and therefore the main developer and chief 'test-pilot' of all these materials.